Courageous Overcomers

CHALLENGE
BIBLE STUDY GUIDES

Old Testament Women by Sara Buswell
   Believers or Beguilers
   Courageous Overcomers
   Vain or Visionary
   Selfless or Selfish

When God Calls by Sara Buswell
   Responding to God's Call
   Submitting to God's Call

The Life of David by Mary Nelle Schaap
   Seeing God in the Life of Young David
   Seeing God in the Life of David the King

Portraits of Jesus from the Gospel Writers by Mary Nelle Schaap
   Portraits of Jesus from Matthew and Mark
   Portraits of Jesus from Luke and John

Studies in Old Testament Poetry by Kathleen Buswell Nielson
   This God We Worship
   Resting Secure

Courageous Overcomers

Old Testament Women

Sara Buswell

BAKER BOOK HOUSE
Grand Rapids, Michigan 49516

© 1993 by Sara Buswell

Published by Baker Books
a division of Baker Book House Company
P.O. Box 6287, Grand Rapids, MI 49516-6287

ISBN: 0-8010-1047-0

Second printing, October 1994

Printed in the United States of America

Chapters in this compilation are taken from *The Challenge of Old Testament Women 1* © 1986 by Baker Book House Company and *The Challenge of Old Testament Women 2* © 1987 by Baker Book House Company.

Unless otherwise indicated, the New International Version is used throughout. Other versions used are the King James Version (KJV) and the Revised Standard Version (RSV).

Contents

Introduction

This book is an invitation to meet women of the Old Testament, and to apply principles of God's character and design seen in them to your own personality and circumstances. The text and study questions are intended to facilitate your acquaintance with these women who, after all, are not very different from yourself. To be a woman today, pleasing to God and transformed to the image of his likeness, is a high calling, a real challenge. But God has not left us without models to warn and to welcome us along the way.

The relevance of each Bible character to the needs of each reader will be different. You may not agree with the applications suggested by other members of your group or in the printed text of this book. That is not important. What matters is that you grow closer to God as you realize that his Word is living and active, and that he desires to make himself known to you personally. As you become acquainted with these women, your relationship with the Lord will deepen as well.

There is always more to discover in God's living Word, even within a narrow range of study. Remember the guidelines and the purpose of your search as we have begun it together. Don't water down the Scriptures or weaken the punch of its message. Let each woman speak from within her own context. With prayer and imagination, put yourself in her situation, and invite God to reveal and apply his relevant principles to your life through her story. Don't indulge in fantasy. Fake jewels have no value, however attractive they may be. The Bible is true, its characters real historical people just as we are. What a privilege we have to know our God, and ourselves, through its study and application. The challenge continues. I pray you will enjoy it and share it as you grow.

Study Plan

1. Read the questions at the beginning of each lesson.

2. Read the Scripture passage(s) listed and be aware of the questions as you read. Allow time to think about words or phrases or incidents that are especially meaningful to you. Underline them in your Bible.

3. Formulate initial answer(s) to questions.

4. If possible, discuss answers with a friend or group.

5. Read the lesson commentary.

6. Revise answers, if necessary.

7. Apply your answers to your life as God directs.

1

Naaman's Maid

Primary Scripture Reading	**Supplementary References**
2 Kings 5	Matthew 18:1–5
	Luke 4:24–27; 9:46–48

Questions for Study and Discussion

1. Who was Naaman, and what was his problem?

   Commander of army, leprous King of Syria -Aram

2. What can you discover about Naaman's maid?

   She cared about his having leprosy

   13409 eager to please

   What did she know about the God of Israel? What did she tell Naaman to do? *a lot - she was from Israel see the prophet in Samaria*

3. What risks did Naaman's maid face in presenting her message? How was she protected? *She spoke to Naaman's wife not Naaman directly. She faced death or being sent back.*

   What have you risked to tell someone about God's saving power?

4. How did the message become distorted in transmission from the maid to her mistress and master, then to the kings of Syria and Israel? How did it get straightened out?

Elisha the prophet intervened

How has God's truth overcome obstacles for you?

5. List the sequence of steps in Naaman's actual cure.

What nearly caused Naaman to miss it? What was the turning point of his life? *His own preconceived idea of how to be healed. His servants changed his attitude*

6. Do you think the relationship of Naaman to his maid was any different after his return? How might she have reacted to his cure? *yes — in humble thanksgiving*

Have you ever played a part in God's miracle of physical or spiritual healing? *No*

7. How can rank affect a person's ability to be an effective agent of God's message?

Consider Naaman's maid in the light of Matthew 18:1–5 and Luke 9:46–48. How does her story encourage and challenge you?

A single verse of Scripture offers a tiny glimpse rather than a full biographical sketch. Without making too much of Naaman's young maid, we can discover in her story several important principles concerning how God's messages are transmitted through his servants. Naaman's servant girl was not a major protagonist in 2 Kings 5, but she did initiate a complex chain of events that culminated in her master's triumphant affirmation of faith.

Truth Bears Fruit

A seed consists of an embryo that contains the reproducible life substance of the plant, to be nourished by the endosperm and protected by an outer covering. This tough skin or shell can take quite a beating without allowing any harm to the embryo inside, so that even after going through an extended period of hardship—such as being in adverse weather, rocky soil, or inadequate moisture—the seed can still germinate when conditions improve. At the beginning of 2 Kings 5 we see the kernel of God's truth, contained within the heart of Naaman's servant girl, still safe after a series of unfavorable circumstances.

> Now Naaman was commander of the army of the king of Aram. He was a great man in the sight of his master and highly regarded, because through him the LORD had given victory to Aram. He was a valiant soldier, but he had leprosy. Now bands from Aram had gone out and had taken captive a young girl from Israel, and she served Naaman's wife (2 Kings 5:1–2).

Note the many obstacles working against this girl's ministry. First, she was an Israelite captive in Syria, the enemy of her people. She was a slave. She was a girl. And she was young. What chance did her message have when it came from someone of the wrong age, sex, rank, religion, and national origin? She risked being ignored, teased, or punished for daring to speak up at all. Yet the truth *persevered* and was heard.

The second obstacle was the limitation of her knowledge of God. To her mistress she said, "If only my master would see the prophet who is in Samaria! He would cure him of his leprosy." But this was not the whole story, not then nor today. God may work through prophets or doctors, through men or medicine, but the power to heal and restore is his alone. The servant girl may have spoken more from partial ignorance or in deference to Elisha's reputation than from her own experience of faith, but she spoke with full assurance, and the truth *penetrated* the darkness to offer the hope that sent Naaman on his way to Israel.

The third obstacle was the number of stages in the transmission of the young girl's message. She spoke with Naaman's wife, who told her husband, who talked to the king of Syria, who sent Naaman with a letter to his enemy the king of Israel. By that time the message read, "With this letter I am sending my servant Naaman to you so that you may cure him of his leprosy." Obviously, something had been lost in translation, as now neither God *nor* his prophet was mentioned, but the king himself was presumed—possibly mockingly—to possess curative powers. No wonder the king panicked! As in the children's game Telephone, some static (here in the form of spiritual deafness or disbelief) distorted or interrupted the connection at one of the "switchboards." The king of Israel, instead of redirecting Naaman in his search for God's healing, tore his robes in desperation and cried out,

> "Am I God? Can I kill and bring back to life? Why does this fellow send someone to me to be cured of his leprosy? See how he is trying to pick a quarrel with me!" (2 Kings 5:7).

A beginning student of electricity learns that current flows only when three things are present: a power source, a load to use the power (lightbulb, motor, etc.), and a conductor, all forming a continuous circuit. Power is cut off from the load when there is a break in the line. When the king of Israel broke the circuit of God's power in Naaman's life, indicating his own lack of insight and faith, God worked through Elisha from the terminal on the other end to reconnect the wires.

> When Elisha the man of God heard that the king of Israel had torn his robes, he sent him this message: "Why have you torn your robes? Have the man come to me and he will know that there is a prophet in Israel" (2 Kings 5:8).

Thus, the transmission of God's power was successfully completed. The life in the seed of truth planted by Naaman's servant girl was *preserved*.

In the same way, when we speak with assurance of that which we know about God, the smallest expression of our faith may become the impetus through which another person discovers the way, the truth, and the life. God's miraculous, life-giving truth can overcome such obstacles as adverse circumstances, ignorance, and interference to persevere, penetrate, and preserve its saving power, for ourselves and for others.

Truth Takes Root

Naaman went to a lot of trouble to get through to God's prophet, and he was furious at Elisha's refusal to see him, not to mention his failure to work magic over him. Naaman's pride in his position and in his own perseverance on this occasion nearly prevented him from accepting God's gift of healing when it required of him no effort or price. Because he at first refused to humble himself by enter-

ing the Jordan River, he almost failed the prophet's test of
humility which must precede faith to bring about a cure.

Many believers have seen in Naaman's story a picture of
how a Christian can accept Christ's free gift of cleansing
and salvation only in a spirit of true submission. God had
protected the little seed of his truth, which the servant girl
planted, through many unfavorable circumstances. Finally,
the conditions began to change. Naaman's heart opened
in obedience and he accepted the prophet's prescription
to wash himself seven times in the Jordan River (at the urging of his servants, we note again). He was physically
restored, spiritually healed. As the water symbolically
reached down into the seed of truth in his heart, new life
and faith burst forth for Naaman. His cognitive response
of faith was as miraculous as the healing itself. Both were
the result of God's grace when he said, "Now I *know* that
there is no God in all the world except in Israel" (2 Kings
5:15, italics added). Having humbled himself by simple
obedience, he went on to real faith in God and so gained
access to the presence of God's prophet at last.

Do we share Naaman's conviction? Francis Schaeffer has
said that only the empty hands of faith can receive the full
measure of God's grace. We must learn to release our hold
on our possessions and our positions, and accept his gift
of eternal life. Psalm 116:12–13 (KJV) says, "What shall I
render unto the LORD for all of his benefits toward me? I
will take the cup of salvation, and call upon the name of
the LORD."

What else does a seed require in order to grow, besides
water and sunshine? Soil, of course, and that is the next
thing Naaman desired.

> "Please let me, your servant, be given as much *earth* as a
> pair of mules can carry, for your servant will never again
> make burnt offerings and sacrifices to any other god but
> the LORD" (2 Kings 5:17, italics added).

Naaman still had much to learn *about* the Lord, but his faith *in* him was securely planted. Undoubtedly, the little servant girl could see the fruit borne of her simple message in her master's changed life, which would in turn nourish her own faith. This cross-pollination of blessings can be a reality in our lives, too, as we grow through sharing with others God's truth, grace, and peace.

The world says show me + I'll believe
Jesus say's Believe + I'll show you

2

Naomi

Primary Scripture Reading	Supplementary References
Ruth 1–4	Luke 22:31–32
	2 Corinthians 12:1–10
	Hebrews 12:1–12

Questions for Study and Discussion

1. Why did Naomi go to Moab?

   What series of events made her decide to return to Bethlehem? What emotions might she have had that influenced her decision?

2. Describe Naomi's relationships with her two daughters-in-law. Why did she urge them both to return to their homes, but later accept Ruth's plea to remain with her?

   How would you differentiate urging from nagging?

3. List the attributes of God that are either stated explicitly or implied in the Book of Ruth.

How did Naomi testify to God's grace during both her good times and bad?

What is your experience with God, and how is your life a witness to others?

4. Was it true that the Lord's hand had gone out against Naomi? How did he also bless her?

How do you reconcile God's power with the presence of evil in the world? Why does he allow his people to suffer?

5. What influence did Naomi have on Ruth?

What influence did Ruth have on Naomi?

How have you been blessed with a similar friendship?

6. Who was Boaz?

List the sequence of events by which Boaz became the kinsman-redeemer.

Did Naomi and Ruth act appropriately or inconsistently with God's plan concerning Boaz?

*S*ome Christians may imagine that we should only speak for the Lord when we are experiencing success in our lives, and that it would be better to remain silent when we are struggling or suffering lest we give God a bad name. We worry that our faith is valuable to others only when it demonstrates our personal victory, and forget that it is Christ's sure and final victory that should always be our focus.

Naomi was not a prophetess, yet her life has a message that is both profound and practical for our day. She experienced extensive personal hardship and endured periods of depression, yet she continued to praise and trust God for his blessings wherever she found them. She was honest in expressing her true feelings, which were not always pleasant, but she never lost all hope. She was sensitive, sincere, unselfish—an ideal mother-in-law. Her witness was winsome; Ruth, her daughter-in-law, was drawn by her beautiful character to share first faith with Naomi, and then her future and her family.

Faith

The Book of Ruth, in which Naomi's story is found, opens with a famine in Judah, during the days when the judges ruled. The nation of Moab had already caused repeated difficulties for Israel (Num. 21–25; Judg. 3). God had warned his people not to have any dealings with the Moabites, and not to marry foreign wives. Nevertheless, when the famine became severe, a man named Elimelech decided to take his wife Naomi and his two sons to Moab, expecting that he could better provide for them there. But he died, and his sons married Moabite women, Orpah and Ruth. About ten years later the sons also died, "and Naomi was left without her two sons and her husband" (Ruth 1:5).

The opening verses of the Book of Ruth suggest that Naomi was not a woman to stir up controversy in her family. She would probably have obeyed quietly when her husband announced the move to Moab, and after his death remained quietly in the home of her sons and their pagan wives. She was not the type to preach at them concerning their disregard of God's directions, nor would she have tried to usurp their authority over their households. If the men had survived, Naomi probably would not have spoken up at all. But while she was quiet, and later when she was alone, she kept her ears and her heart open for news of God's work.

> When she heard in Moab that the LORD had come to the aid of his people by providing food for them, Naomi and her daughters-in-law prepared to return home from there (Ruth 1:6).

Thus, two events put Naomi back on the road to her home in Bethlehem: the deaths of her husband and sons, and the report of God's provision for his people in Judah. There was nothing to keep her in Moab any longer, and every reason for her to return to Judah.

For Orpah and Ruth the decision was much more difficult. They had spent more than ten years with Naomi, and they undoubtedly felt very close to her as well as obligated to continue caring for their mother-in-law. However, their own family and national ties were in Moab; they would not have been eager to live as widows and foreigners in

Judah, no matter how much they loved Naomi. Naomi's gentle sensitivity to these mixed emotions was manifest when she allowed Orpah and Ruth to start out on the journey with her.

> Then Naomi said to her two daughters-in-law, "Go back, each of you, to your mother's house. May the LORD show kindness to you, as you have shown to your dead and to me. May the LORD grant that each of you will find rest in the home of another husband" (Ruth 1:8–9).

The younger women wept aloud and insisted on going with her, but Naomi overruled them once again.

> But Naomi said, "Return home, my daughters. Why would you come with me? Am I going to have any more sons, who could become your husbands? Return home, my daughters; I am too old to have another husband. Even if I thought there was still hope for me—even if I had a husband tonight and then gave birth to sons—would you wait until they grew up? No, my daughters. It is more bitter for me than for you, because the LORD's hand has gone out against me" (Ruth 1:11–13).

This time the two daughters-in-law responded differently from each other according to their contrasting temperaments. At first both women were prepared to go with Naomi out of a sense of duty and affection, but at Naomi's urging, Orpah turned back. We presume she remained in Moab with her own family, and perhaps married again, as Naomi had prayed she would. The Bible tells us nothing more about her. But Ruth persisted. Consider what must have been the tremendous impact of Naomi's life on Ruth during their years together, which moved Ruth to respond with these beautiful words:

"Don't urge me to leave you or to turn back from you. Where you go I will go, and where you stay I will stay. Your people will be my people and your God my God. Where you die I will die, and there I will buried. May the LORD deal with me, be it ever so severely, if anything but death separates you and me" (Ruth 1:16–17).

Naomi knew when to urge and when to stop urging. Three times she tried to persuade the women to stay in Moab. Orpah accepted the offer because it was reasonable, sensitive, and sincere. But Ruth was different. She said, "Don't urge me to leave." Naomi's sensitivity is shown once again in verse 18: "When Naomi realized that Ruth was determined to go with her, she stopped urging her." Instead of selfishly pushing her own preferences onto her daughters-in-law, Naomi watched and listened for signs of their true inclinations.

Naomi was not trying to outmaneuver or overpower her daughters-in-law. She simply allowed God to work through her life to touch them. Orpah and Ruth each had the same opportunity to become acquainted with God through Naomi's deep faith displayed in her day-to-day existence. But the seed fell on different kinds of soil (see Matt. 13). Orpah returned to her people and her gods; Ruth said, "Your people will be my people and your God my God."

If we sincerely ask God to use our lives to bear eternal fruit for him in the lives of others, we, too, must recognize the fact that some people will respond with open hearts while others will refuse the good news we want to share. We must be available, but also accepting of the time, methods, or people he chooses to relay his message (see 1 Cor. 3:5–9). Naomi could have become discouraged over her 50 percent failure in bringing her daughters-in-law to the Lord. Instead, she accepted each of their decisions without judgment or remorse.

When Naomi arrived in Bethlehem with Ruth, her former friends barely recognized her. "Can this be Naomi?" they wondered. Once again, Naomi's testimony was hardly triumphant, but it did express her deep awareness of God's activity in her life during her long absence from home.

> "Don't call me Naomi," she told them. "Call me Mara, because the Almighty has made my life very bitter. I went away full, but the LORD has brought me back empty. Why call me Naomi? The LORD has afflicted me; the Almighty has brought misfortune upon me" (Ruth 1:20–21).

What kind of winsome witness was this? It was honest. Through her trials in Moab—the deaths of her husband and sons, as well as their struggles to find food in a foreign land—Naomi had come to feel that the LORD's hand had gone out against her, which she had told Orpah and Ruth and repeated to her friends in Bethlehem. But she still felt that it was God's hand at work. There was real bitterness, to the point that Naomi requested that she be called Mara, which means "bitter," instead of her own name, which means "pleasant."

But Naomi never denied God's existence nor rejected the possibility of his blessing for others or herself at a later time. She saw no contradiction in her belief that God, who sometimes afflicted, was also the one who provided and blessed. This truth had been verified by her experiences. Because Naomi was honest in sharing her sufferings, her friends were able to share all the more in her ultimate success, which we shall see at the end of her story.

Fantasy

Think for a moment about Naomi's statement that God's hand had gone out against her. Was this mere fantasy, proof that her temporary depression was becoming paranoia?

Can God's hand ever go against one of his people, or is it only Satan who brings misfortune and evil into the world? Do we not have one adversary and one advocate? How can our friend become our enemy?

The Bible has a great deal to teach on these crucial questions, more than we can explore in depth here. But we know that God is omnipotent, and that the domain of his power is not limited to working only in behalf of those who honor him. He has "set his hand," "kindled his anger," and "raised up enemies" against hundreds of individuals and nations who have rebelled against him, whether or not they were numbered among his chosen people. For example, see 1 Samuel 7:13 and Isaiah 5:25.

God sometimes does allow bad things to happen to his people today also, not for his own pleasure nor for our punishment, but always in perfect harmony with his character and purposes. We may feel the impact of these blows as a result of our deliberate choice to disregard or disobey God's authority over our lives, or we may simply become wounded in the crossfire as the battle rages around us in the world. None of us is immune. God knows that Satan desires to sift us like wheat (Luke 22:31–32) and he may give him limited permission to do so, as he did with Job, in order to bring us back into full commitment and service to himself. Romans 8:28 does not mean that our walk with God will necessarily always be in the sunshine.

Naomi was not accusing God of being mean to her; she was acknowledging that he was in control of her life and that she had suffered. This challenges us to honestly and realistically acknowledge the status of our walk with God, no matter how he may be dealing with us at the moment. Doing so is a more powerful testimony to his presence than any evangelistic formula we can recite. To have deep doubts and serious needs does not mean that our faith is weak. But faith does then become visible to ourselves as well as to others; for when we are most vulnerable we are also most transparent, and the often-painful process of God's tender dealing with his children is most readily observed. We must be willing to become small and to hurt in order to grow and be healed. Naomi's apparent weakness did not weaken her witness.

The connection between our pain and our praise does not mean that God wants us to rejoice over our sufferings *per se*, any more than we should rejoice over the sufferings of other people, which would be dishonest and cruel. But he does want us to rejoice in *him*. Always (Phil. 4:4–7). Amazingly, we find that we can endure any agony when we know God is with us in it, supplying his strength and love even when we do not comprehend his plan.

Naomi's attitude was both honest and contagious, and Ruth caught it. She was determined to share Naomi's life and faith, as indeed she already had. Her vow, "May the LORD deal with me, be it ever so severely, if anything but death separates you and me," was proof of her conversion. Naomi had not promised Ruth a life of ease, nor had she lived one. Ruth must have watched Naomi suffer and must have drawn on her strength through the years they had already shared. Naomi's sustaining faith in God had obviously impressed Ruth and brought her into fellowship with her Lord.

Throughout the Book of Ruth God's name is upheld as a source of life and blessing. Of the eighty-four verses in the book, sixteen speak of the Lord, either in affirmation or supplication. They tell that he provided food, showed kindness, gave offspring, enabled Ruth to conceive, and provided Naomi with a kinsman-redeemer; that he was asked to show kindness, to grant rest with new homes and husbands for Orpah and Ruth, to be with and to bless Boaz and his field workers, and to repay and reward Ruth for her kindness to Naomi; and that Ruth and Boaz each made a vow in the name of the Lord. Naomi's faith in an active, present, real, personal God permeates the story of Ruth and reaches out to our hearts as well. Can we say that others have "come to take refuge" under the wings of the Lord because of the honest, vibrant messages of our lives?

Future and Family

When Ruth linked herself to Naomi by faith, she made a commitment to share the future with her, whatever happened. From that time on they functioned as a harmonious team. Chapter 2 of Ruth explains how their partnership developed. Ruth offered to glean, and Naomi approved. Ruth was successful working in Boaz's fields, and shared with Naomi not only the grain she had gathered but also the leftovers from the lunch Boaz had given her. Naomi was ready with words of praise to God for his providence and with encouragement and advice for Ruth. The two women lived in this way for some time, with Ruth working in the fields and Naomi managing their home. They seemed content; Naomi's outbursts of bitterness disappeared as she began to rest in God's care and Ruth's companionship.

From the start, when Naomi had set out for Bethlehem from Moab, she had made it clear to her daughters-in-law that the chances of providing husbands for them from her own family were nil. Nevertheless, Ruth insisted on remaining with Naomi, her people, and her God until death, without mentioning any desire for a husband or children of her own. When Naomi and Ruth settled down in Bethlehem, both of them expected to remain single.

But Naomi was still open to receive news of God's work. Just as she had once heard that he had come to the aid of his people in providing food, she began to realize that he might be coming to her aid once again in providing a kinsman-redeemer for her family. When she heard how kind Boaz had been to Ruth, a foreigner, in inquiring about her, protecting her, and making her task easier, as well as providing her lunch, Naomi praised God not only for his kindness but also for his kinship.

> "The Lord bless him!" Naomi said to her daughter-in-law. "The Lord has not stopped his kindness to the living and the dead." She added, "That man is our close relative; he is one of our kinsman-redeemers" (Ruth 2:20).

Neither Ruth nor Naomi was a schemer who selfishly plotted to trap Boaz into marriage. But they were available to cooperate with God. The fact that Ruth "just happened" to work in Boaz's fields and to find favor in his eyes encouraged Naomi to suggest that God might have a greater purpose in mind. Similarly, when we trust in God, our eyes are opened to recognize his design in events that may appear to others to be mere coincidence.

Naomi gave Ruth careful instructions in how to approach Boaz at night on the threshing floor, which she obeyed perfectly. Boaz, too, was sensitive to God's leading, and as Naomi had predicted to Ruth, he did not let the matter rest until it was settled. The role of kinsman-redeemer included the right to redeem (buy) the land of a deceased relative, with the condition that offspring would be raised in his name so that no branch of a family would be cut off from property and heritage. Boaz offered the right of redeeming Mahlon's land and widow to the one individual more eligible to act than he. When this man declined, Boaz happily served as the kinsman-redeemer himself; he married Ruth, and their son Obed became the lawful heir of the land belonging to Naomi's husband and sons. His name continued the family line, and in fact he was a link in Christ's genealogy (see Matt. 1:5). Ruth's future and family were thus secured forever, and her name is recorded with honor in God's Word. Naomi's life's message had brought Ruth into God's family; Ruth in turn brought new life into Naomi's family. Now Naomi's friends could truly rejoice with her over her new son.

Even when she felt that God had dealt harshly with her, Naomi sought to know his will. Her discouragement never became disbelief. She kept her emotions in line with her sure knowledge of God. Because she did not hide her weakness, her strength strengthened others.

In our day, which stresses total openness in relationships, perhaps Christians have become too self-conscious and too fearful of being accused of hypocrisy. If we're not actually bubbling over with joy in the Lord at every moment, we hesitate to recommend him to others, and fail to appreciate his activity in the world around us. "Our walk must reflect our talk," we say, so we keep silent. "We cannot lead where we have never traveled," we mutter, and remain motionless. Satan is having a field day tying our tongues and hobbling our feet. "Praise the Lord, anyhow," is a popular but sadly feeble effort at Christian encouragement. Dear friends, we are missing myriad opportunities to glorify our God for his everlasting greatness and goodness! We need to learn from Naomi. While she was aware that her afflictions came from the Lord, her importance to him was affirmed by his lovingkindness.

Perhaps you have gone away full and come back empty in some aspect of your life. As you honestly evaluate your present position, whatever the pain, can you trust that God is not yet finished? Do not close your heart or your ears to his voice, to news of the work he will yet do, to the fruit of his love and fulfillment of your life still ahead. And meanwhile, freely tell others how God is working in your life right now. They will very likely be drawn closer to him through your truthful testimony.

3

Ruth

Primary Scripture Reading	Supplementary References
Book of Ruth	Genesis 19
	Numbers 25
	Judges 3
	Matthew 1:5
	John 14:15
	Romans 8:28
	Philippians 2:5–11
	Colossians 3:23–24

Questions for Study and Discussion

1. Read and enjoy the whole Book of Ruth. Which people did Ruth obey, and how often?   *Moabite customs*
   Mahlon, naomi

   Of what significance is the fact that she was not an Israelite but a Moabite? What other factors might have made it difficult for Ruth to obey Naomi?

2. Describe your relationship to your in-laws, other relatives, friends, or co-workers to whom you are responsible. How does it compare with that of Ruth and Naomi?

What principles underlying their relationship could you apply to your situation, and with what positive results?

3. Compare Orpah's response to Naomi with that of Ruth. Which course do you think you might have taken, and why?

When have you obeyed either minimally or maximally, and with what results?

Under what conditions do you find obedience fulfilling or frustrating?

4. How do you connect the requirement of obedience to God with obedience to people, both in principle and in your practical experience?

Do you think your attitude or act of obedience has served as a testimony to a relative or friend?

How have you used Christ's example of submission to strengthen or comfort you?

5. What about the men in this story? Do you think Elimelech acted obediently in his decision to go to Moab in the first place?

   What happened for good or for bad as a result?

6. Give several instances that demonstrate Boaz's obedience to God throughout this story. How did this character trait encourage Ruth to obey both him and God?

   Briefly describe some key men or women in your life who impressed you by their obedience to God and tell how this has helped develop the trait of obedience in you.

7. Do you find any negative qualities in Ruth's character?

   How can you apply the outstanding experiences in her life to your own situation?

   List several blessings Ruth received for her obedience. How have you been similarly blessed?

Mahlon — sickly
Chillion — wasting

*R*uth and Esther are the only two books in the Bible named for women, and both have much to teach us about obedience. In our own time, when the role of mother-in-law is widely mocked and daughters-in-law are often disrespectful, the model relationship between Ruth and Naomi is especially valuable. But Ruth's story is more than a handbook on how to get along with one's in-laws. It celebrates the gentle beauty of love and loyalty between individuals, and it demonstrates the positive power of obedience to God for both personal fulfillment and wider blessing. By committing herself to Naomi as well as to Naomi's God, Ruth found satisfaction in service. Instead of losing her identity by her voluntary and complete submission, Ruth's place was joyfully confirmed.

Surprising Obedience

The harmony between Ruth and her mother-in-law is even more appealing when we consider two unusual factors that could have driven them apart:

> Now Elimelech, Naomi's husband, died, and she was left with her two sons. They married Moabite women, one named Orpah and the other Ruth. After they had lived there about ten years, both Mahlon and Kilion also died, and Naomi was left without her two sons and her husband (Ruth 1:3–5).

Mahlon, the natural connecting link between Ruth and Naomi, was dead. Nothing specific is mentioned about the way the two women got along with each other while he was alive during those ten years in Moab. Instead, the account begins with the development of their relationship after Mahlon's death and at the time of the women's departure for Judah. This fact invites me to consider my relationship with my mother-in-law. Do we function together only because of and through the mediation of my husband, her son? Or can we develop a friendship for its own sake, one of wide and lasting substance for our mutual benefit that goes beyond our having Jamie in common?

The second potentially divisive factor was that Ruth was a Moabite. A brief review of the history of this neighboring nation proves that its land and people were clearly off limits for the Hebrews. The founding father Moab was the result of Lot's incestuous union with his older daughter (Gen. 19:37). Though Moab was not on the list of nations to be entirely destroyed by the Israelites under Joshua, its idolatrous practices were particularly offensive and troublesome (Num. 25). Judges 3 relates that Eglon, king of Moab, received power from the Lord to punish Israel for eighteen years. When his people again cried out to him, God raised up the judge Ehud, who killed Eglon and defeated Moab, thus establishing peace for eighty years.

The Book of Ruth begins, "In the days when the judges ruled," placing it within this period. Elimelech's decision to take his family into Moab to escape the famine in Israel probably occurred at a time when Moab was subdued, or at least not openly hostile toward Israel. Nevertheless, God had repeatedly warned the Israelites not to mingle, intermarry, or otherwise join in the wicked practices of alien nations. The fact that both Naomi's sons chose Moabite women for wives shows that they did not heed these instructions, if indeed they had received them. It also indicates the attractiveness of these foreign influences to the Israelites, a temptation from which God desired to shield them. But we also see his mercy in grafting into his line of blessing one Moabite because of her faith and obedience.

Naomi had two daughters-in-law, Ruth and Orpah. In view of their position as Moabite widows, it may seem that Orpah's decision to return to her own mother's house was more natural than Ruth's when Naomi announced her determination to go back to Bethlehem. We might even argue that Orpah, after politely offering to accompany Naomi, was acting in accord with her mother-in-law's wishes by remaining in Moab with her own people. Ruth, on the other hand, "clung to her" and stubbornly refused to leave Naomi. But Orpah's obedience can only be called superficial, or minimal. Her offer was made out of duty, not devotion, and Naomi discerned and declined it as such. Orpah's name means "stubbornness," and nothing more is said of her after she kissed Naomi farewell. In contrast, Ruth, whose name means "friendship," remained to finish her story and claim a place in the genealogy of David and ultimately of Christ (Matt. 1:5).

Witness in Obedience

Ruth did more than merely remain with Naomi; she was in fact her main support, both during their journey and after their arrival in Israel, even though she was the stranger in Bethlehem. News of her faithfulness circulated quickly and preceded her into the fields of Boaz. When she asked why he was being so kind to a foreigner, Boaz replied,

> "I've been told all about what you have done for your mother-in-law since the death of your husband—how you left your father and mother and your homeland and came to live with a people you did not know before" (Ruth 2:11).

Though directly attracted by her outward beauty and manner, Boaz was already aware of her reputation for loyal love and service. Boaz told her, "All my fellow townsmen know that you are a woman of noble character" (Ruth 3:11).

Here we see the powerful testimony of Ruth's relationship with Naomi. Her unselfish devotion to one person, characterized by her obedience, made her appealing to another person and to a whole community. However, Ruth did not flaunt her obedience as long-suffering, but held it in her heart as love. She was not looking for praise or pity, and she seemed surprised that her service had been observed. Not once did she begrudge Naomi's leadership or bemoan her own circumstances. Instead of bitterness there was beauty, in her attitude as well as on her face. Ruth found her obedience fulfilling. Her immediate and ultimate rewards far exceeded anything she could have anticipated or desired.

Wholeness of Obedience

How did Ruth's obedience come to have such a tremendous impact on those around her? It started with a personal commitment, a permanent decision that brought her peace and provided her with direction for all that followed. On the boundary of Moab, Ruth had told Naomi,

> "Don't urge me to leave you or turn back from you. Where you go I will go, and where you stay I will stay. Your people will be my people and your God my God. Where you die I will die, and there I will be buried. May the LORD deal with me, be it ever so severely, if anything but death separates you and me" (Ruth 1:16–17).

This was not a marriage vow; yet, how many of us have used these words in our own weddings, and how strong our families would be if we lived them! In my case, I married my husband because his God had become my God, and so we could commit our life together into his care.

Ruth's commitment was absolute. Rather than constraining her, it created new purpose and opportunity for developing her character. When they arrived in Bethlehem, Ruth volunteered to glean, saying, "Let me go to the fields and pick up the leftover grain behind anyone in whose eyes I find favor" (Ruth 2:2). Naomi accepted with the simple words, "Go ahead, my daughter." When she returned, Ruth shared her grain with Naomi and gave an account of the day's events. Then it was Naomi who sensed God's direction and gave Ruth detailed instructions as to how to approach Boaz, which Ruth obeyed with perfect results (Ruth 3:1–6). Ruth 4:17 indicates that after Ruth's future and family were secure, Naomi was included in the household redeemed by Boaz, for when the neighbors noticed how much she cared for Obed they said, "Naomi has a son." Truly, the deepest love, trust, and respect were at the center of the relationship of these women, which brought their mutual fulfillment.

As Ruth obeyed Naomi, so she obeyed Boaz, both at their first meeting and later at the threshing floor. She won the admiration of both Naomi and Boaz as much by the quickness of her unquestioning responses as by her completeness in carrying out commands.

Although I believe that my own children are entitled to know my good reasons behind instructions I give them, sometimes it comes as a delightful surprise to find them trusting my wisdom and benevolence enough to accept my orders without demanding "Why?" But then, haven't we all said to other people, as I certainly have on occasion, "Of course I'm willing to help, but you'll have to tell me *why* you want it done this way"? We measure out our cooperation in proportion to our understanding of and agreement with their desires. Isn't it refreshing and challenging to find no such spirit in Ruth? She won respect because she offered her respect in the form of obedience.

Worship by Obedience

The product of Ruth's obedience was Obed, the child fathered by Boaz as kinsman-redeemer, the one who would inherit the family land and name in place of Naomi's deceased husband and sons. Obed means "worship" in

Hebrew. Is not obedience really the outward action that derives from the inner response of faith, love, and trust practiced in regard to individuals and ultimately God? Christ said, "If you love me, you will obey what I command" (John 14:15). Ruth's acts of obedience throughout her story may be interpreted as practical acts of worship of the God she had made her own by faith.

In this light we must evaluate our obedience toward those in positions of authority over us. Is it freely offered? Is it maximal like Ruth's, or minimal like Orpah's? If we are afraid to yield in obedience to another person, we can draw comfort and confidence from the Lord himself, knowing that he can be fully trusted in all things to work "for the good of those who love him, who have been called according to his purpose" (Rom. 8:28). Realizing that it is God who controls every aspect of our lives, are we not safe in his hands, and in the hands of those whom by his sovereign will we are directed to obey?

But let us be honest. Some people are easier to obey than others, either because of their personalities or ours. We are not always free to choose whom and when we are to obey. Perhaps the situation is difficult, one in which submission is demanded when trust has not yet been established. Instead of dwelling on the shortcomings of people who wield authority, we do well to yield to God's perfect love, faithfulness, and trustworthiness. Remember that Jesus did not hold himself above obedience, but gave his life in demonstration of total submission to his Father.

Your attitude should be the same as that of Christ Jesus:

Who, being in very nature God, did not consider equality with God something to be grasped,
but made himself nothing, taking the very nature of a servant, being made in human likeness.

And being found in appearance as a man, he humbled himself and became obedient to death—even death on a
cross!
Therefore God exalted him to the highest place and gave
him the name that is above every name,
that at the name of Jesus every knee should bow, in heaven
and on earth and under the earth,
and every tongue confess that Jesus Christ is Lord, to the
glory of God the Father (Phil. 2:5–11).

As Christ did, as Ruth did, let us ask God to work in us
to transform our feeble gestures of human obedience into
acts of divine worship. We can find delight in serving the
Lord, instead of indulging in resentment over subservient
relationships. The result will be inner freedom and release
from bitterness, and also a powerful testimony to those
exercising authority and to outside observers as well. Just
as Ruth's attitude of obedience toward Naomi moved Boaz
and all Bethlehem, the Holy Spirit will enable us to move
others. Paul taught the church at Colosse:

Whatever you do, work at it with all your heart, as working for the Lord, not for men, since you know that you will
receive an inheritance from the Lord as a reward. It is the
Lord Christ you are serving (Col. 3:23–24).

While we obey others we can joyfully remember that it
is God alone who is worthy of complete obedience. When
our confidence in him is reflected in our submission to others we become living testimonies to our trust in God's perfect plan. If we follow Ruth's beautiful example, someone
may examine our stories and find the witness, the whole-
ness, and the worship in our lives of obedience.

4

Sarah

Primary Scripture Reading

Genesis 11–23

Supplementary References

Deuteronomy 28:9–10
Ezekiel 36:23–36
John 3:5–8
Ephesians 2:1–10; 5:22–33
Hebrews 11:6–19
1 Peter 3:1–7

Questions for Study and Discussion

1. Skim the Genesis chapters, noting highlights of Sarah's life, particularly her name change in chapter 17. What was Sarah's greatest desire? What did she decide to do about it? Whose help did she solicit?

   What were the immediate and long-range consequences of her effort?

   Does God need your help in order to fulfill his Word, and if so, what kind of help?

   He doesn't need my help
   He needs my heart

2. Why did God change Abram's name to Abraham, and Sarai's to Sarah (Gen. 17:5, 15)? Do you find any resulting changes in their personalities or conduct?

   How has God quickened you, in the sense of giving you new life, since you have become identified with his name?

3. In Genesis 12 and 20, Abraham told Sarah to lie to two heathen rulers. What was the lie, and how serious were the consequences in each instance? What was Abraham forgetting?

   How do you think you would handle a similar situation in which your spouse, parent, or boss wanted you to tell a lie to protect him or her?

4. Genesis 18:15 relates that Sarah told another lie, which was not prompted by her husband. What was the situation? Why did she lie?

   What did she learn from this experience?

5. What differences do you detect between Abraham's laughter in Genesis 17:17 and Sarah's laughter in 18:12?

Why did they name their baby Isaac?

it means laughter

When have you laughed in response to God's promises? Did you laugh because of joy or unbelief? What happened?

6. Compare Genesis 16:4–6 with 21:8–13. If God told your spouse to do whatever you said (as he told Abraham to do in the second passage), what responsibility would that put on you? How did this command work out for Abraham and Sarah?

Considering the relationship between this husband and wife, why, do you think, did Peter suggest Sarah as a model for wives because she "obeyed Abraham, calling him lord" (1 Peter 3:1–6)?

7. List as many of God's promises to Abraham and Sarah as you can find. What does the New Testament say about their response to the promises?

What promises of God are you claiming for your present situation? Are you expecting a miracle?

How can you demonstrate your faith and obedience to God in seemingly impossible circumstances?

*L*aughter, the Best Medicine" is more than a popular feature in *Reader's Digest*—it describes common experience. But did you know that laughter can also be a symptom of serious spiritual disorder?

God used laughter at a crucial moment in Sarah's life to uncover a root of bitterness and unbelief and to promote the healing process of submission. If we could chart her growth from expedience to obedience, we would note several ups and downs rather than a steady curve. This holds true even after God changed the names of Abram and Sarai to Abraham and Sarah, symbolizing with the Hebrew letter *h* the Spirit's breathing life into their beings. Although they gradually came to understand more of God's promises and power, Sarah and Abraham occasionally reverted to a former level of selfishness and lack of faith through fear. The laughter occurred at the midpoint of their development, and was in response to God's personal revelation.

We might like to think that from the moment God changed Sarah and Abraham's names, or from the time when the Holy Spirit first enters a believer today, there should be no further problems with the old nature—that the switch from villainy to victory should be instantaneous and permanent. But this ideal is no more true for us than it was for Sarah and Abraham; and rightly so, for the concept of obedience includes a real choice at every step. Each one of us has the same potential as they for either fruitfulness or failure, for we sometimes depend on God and sometimes on our own ambitions and abilities to gain our desires.

No Laughing Matter

Abram and Sarai had a serious problem, which is mentioned at the onset and repeated during their history to show its importance:

Terah became the father of Abram, Nahor, and Haran. . . .
Abram and Nahor both married. The name of Abram's wife
was Sarai. . . . Now Sarai was barren; she had no children
(Gen. 11:27–30).

Now Sarai, Abram's wife, had borne him no children (Gen.
16:1).

Ten years had elapsed between these two statements, and
fourteen years more were to pass before Sarah finally, at
age ninety, gave birth to Isaac. In her culture a lack of children was considered equivalent to a lack of favor with God.
Prosperity was measured as much by the size of one's family as by material possessions (see Ps. 127:3–5). Even
though Abram had by this time accumulated great wealth
"in livestock and in silver and gold" (Gen. 13:2), he still
had no offspring. What was the point of material expan-
sion if there would be no future generation in whom to
invest this treasure?

More confusing was the fact that God kept promising
Abram an heir; in fact, he promised him many nations and
rich blessings. Was God delaying out of weakness and
needed Abram and Sarai's help to accomplish his purposes
by any and all means? Or was he perhaps waiting for Abram
and Sarai to show some initiative before he would act in
their behalf? Does God help those who help themselves,
or only those who depend solely on his help? Did the way
in which God gradually unfolded his plans serve as an invitation to their further faith and friendship, or did it continue to simply tease and frustrate Abram and Sarai? How
can we apply God's power and promises today, and what
does he ask of us in return for his favor?

Let us look at the sequence of God's promises to Abram
and Sarai and consider whether they laid claim to them or
contradicted them by their actions. We will also examine

the relationship between Abram and Sarai as a model of support and submission within marriage.

First, God said,

> "Leave your country, your people and your father's household and go to the land I will show you.
>
> I will make you into a great nation and I will bless you;
> I will make your name great, and you will be a blessing.
> I will bless those who bless you, and whoever curses you
>   I will curse;
> and all peoples on earth will be blessed through you"
>   (Gen. 12:1–3).

Later he elaborated concerning the offspring and the land of promise. Even with these assurances, Abram was still unsure about the way in which God would fulfill his word, so he asked about it.

> But Abram said, "O Sovereign LORD, what can you give me since I remain childless and the one who will inherit my estate is Eliezer of Damascus?" And Abram said, "You have given me no children, so a servant in my household will be my heir" (Gen. 15:2–3).

Notice the hint of impatience and the wrong conclusion Abram drew as to what God intended. Therefore, God added,

> "This man will not be your heir, but a son coming from your own body will be your heir." He took him outside and said, "Look at the heavens and count the stars—if indeed you can count them." Then he said to him, "So shall your offspring be" (Gen. 15:4–5).

In response to this promise, Abram finally released his fear and placed his faith in God. "Abram believed the LORD, and he credited it to him as righteousness" (Gen. 15:6).

God then confirmed his covenant and Abram's faith by sending a "smoking fire pot with a blazing torch" to pass between two piles of sacrificed animals, sealing the contract unilaterally. Then he gave a detailed prophecy:

> "Know for certain that your descendants will be strangers in a country not their own, and they will be enslaved and mistreated four hundred years. But I will punish the nation they serve as slaves, and afterward they will come out with great possessions. You, however, will go to your fathers in peace and be buried at a good old age. . . . To your descendants I give this land, from the river of Egypt to the great river, the Euphrates. . . ." (Gen. 15:13–21).

The promise was now very specific, but there was still no mention of Abram's marriage partner. Sadly, almost reproachfully, Sarai concluded that she was not to be an active participant in producing the promised seed through her own body. Notice the beginning of chapter 16:

> Now Sarai, Abram's wife, had borne him no children. But she had an Egyptian maidservant named Hagar; so she said to Abram, "The LORD has kept me from having children. Go, sleep with my maidservant; perhaps I can build a family through her" (Gen. 16:1–2).

Thus, impatience gave way to expedience as Sarai resorted to her own methods and resources to produce a child according to the flesh. We may sympathize with her innocence or ignorance in not knowing the miracle God yet had in store for her, but we cannot really justify the fact that she never asked him for clarification or comfort. Hagar conceived and bore the child Ishmael, and learned an important lesson in submission when she was confronted by "the God who sees me" (Gen. 16:13).

But Sarai was still barren. The only fruits of her self-effort were jealousy, bitterness, blames, and cruelty, which came after Abram abdicated his authority with the words, "Your servant is in your hands. . . . Do with her whatever you think best" (Gen. 16:6). It would take thirteen years of silence in the Scripture record before they were ready for God's next revelation of himself and the miracle of his life-giving power. Each of us would do well to examine our own actions for traces of self-centered expedience rather than full obedience to God.

Today it is just as difficult to know when to take initiative and when to wait expectantly for the fulfillment of God's promises as it was for Abraham and Sarah. Without knowing the future or being able to control all of the factors affecting the behaviors of everyone involved in a decision, how can we choose correctly among alternatives? How can I know what God wants me to do or not to do? That is the question facing all of us and, praise God, we can have help and hope to find the answers, if we ask ourselves:

1. Are my motives self-seeking or God-serving? Am I acting out of fear or faith, pride or praise to God? Am I really trying to gain something for myself or to give all the glory to God?
2. Are my methods consistent with God's character and standards as revealed in his Word? Am I applying appropriate Scripture principles to my situation?
3. Have I asked God to guide me through specific answers to prayer and the comforting peace of the Holy Spirit (Phil. 4:6–7)? How can I monitor the situation and modify my actions as God directs?

If I consider the why, what, and how of my actions in this way, I can be confident that God will rebuke or rescue me if I misstep, and that he will protect and prosper my walk of obedience.

Laughing Place

For years I puzzled over the fact that when Abraham laughed in response to God's renewal of the covenant and promise of a child to Sarah, he was met with an assurance of God's blessing for Ishmael and a repetition of the covenant with Isaac (Gen. 17:17). But Sarah laughed in almost the same way when she heard the promise concerning her son, and she was rebuked. Why did the Lord rebuke one and reward the other for the same natural reaction? The answer may be found in the heart's response to God in these two individuals, and in the position each one took when he spoke to them. Let us place the texts side by side. In chapter 17, we read in part:

> When Abram was ninety-nine years old, the LORD appeared to him and said, "I am God Almighty; walk before me and be blameless. I will confirm my covenant between me and you and will greatly increase your numbers." Abram fell facedown, and God said to him, "As for me, this is my covenant with you: You will be the father of many nations. No longer will you be called Abram; your name will be Abraham, for I have made you a father of many nations. . . . As for you, you must keep my covenant, you and your descendants after you for the generations to come. This is my covenant you are to keep: Every male among you shall be circumcised. . . . God also said to Abraham, "As for Sarai your wife, you are no longer to call her Sarai; her name will be Sarah. I will bless her and will surely give you a son by her. I will bless her so that she will be the mother of nations; kings of peoples will come from her." Abraham fell facedown; he laughed and said to himself, "Will a son be born to a man a hundred years old? Will Sarah bear a child at the age of ninety?" And Abraham said to God, "If only Ishmael might live under your blessing!" Then God said, "Yes, but your wife Sarah will bear you a son, and you will call him Isaac. I will establish my covenant with him as an everlasting covenant for his descendants after him. And as for

Ishmael, I have heard you: I will surely bless him. . . . But my covenant I will establish with Isaac, whom Sarah will bear to you by this time next year" (Gen. 17:1–21).

In chapter 18, Abraham offered hospitality to three visitors who turned out to be two angels and the Lord himself:

While they ate, he stood near them under a tree. "Where is your wife Sarah?" they asked him. "There, in the tent," he said. Then the LORD said, "I will surely return to you about this time next year, and Sarah your wife will have a son." Now Sarah was listening at the entrance to the tent, which was behind him. Abraham and Sarah were already old and well advanced in years, and Sarah was past the age of childbearing. So Sarah laughed to herself as she thought, "After I am worn out and my master is old, will I now have this pleasure?" Then the LORD said to Abraham, "Why did Sarah laugh and say, 'Will I really have a child, now that I am old?' Is anything too hard for the LORD? I will return to you at the appointed time next year and Sarah will have a son." Sarah was afraid, so she lied and said, "I did not laugh." But he said, "Yes, you did laugh" (Gen. 18:8–15).

The notes of cynicism and fear in Sarah's laughter and lie are absent from Abraham's response. He expressed, "Wow!" while she seemed to say, "Hah!" The underlying question was the same for both of them: How could such a thing happen after so long a time? But their expectations and their postures were opposite. Abraham fell facedown in reverent submission, while Sarah stood at the tent door in disbelief. It was no surprise to Abraham that God could read his mind and respond to his inner laughter—that was the way in which God had always communicated with his friend. But stunned silence prevailed when Sarah finally and fully absorbed the fact that here before her was God himself, who could penetrate to the very core of her private pain, giving her the ability to fully trust him at the same time as he enabled her to bear life. Hebrews 11:6 states, "And without faith it is impossible to please God, because anyone who comes to him must believe that he exists and that he rewards those who earnestly seek him."

Sarah did not really seek the Lord until she stopped looking for solutions to her problems within herself; when she sought him, he found her and brought her to himself in full faith and in fulfillment of all his promises. Do not we, too, think some things are too hard for the Lord, or too small for him to bother with?

Laughing Boy

A promise has value only if it is believed and kept. Enjoy the joy bubbling through Sarah and Abraham over the birth of Isaac, whose name means "laughter."

Now the Lord was gracious to Sarah as he had said, and the LORD did for Sarah what he had promised. Sarah became pregnant and bore a son to Abraham in his old age, at the very time God had promised him. Abraham gave the name Isaac to the son Sarah bore him. When his son Isaac was eight days old, Abraham circumcised him, as God commanded him. Abraham was a hundred years old when his son Isaac was born to him. Sarah said, "God has brought me laughter, and everyone who hears about this will laugh with me." And she added, "Who would have said to Abraham that Sarah would nurse children? Yet I have borne him a son in his old age" (Gen. 21:1–7).

When we fully recognize God as our Lord, and receive his Spirit by faith, we can join fully in Sarah's laughter.

We have seen that obedience to God requires faith *in* God. The real miracle of Isaac's birth was the quickening of faith that enabled Abraham and Sarah to generate new life from their old bodies. Similarly, our faith in God's faithfulness to fulfill his promises gives us the power and the purpose for obedience. Without such faith we have neither the reason nor the resource to obey. Ezekiel 36:36 affirms the basis of our faith: "I the LORD have spoken, and I will do it!" And 1 Thessalonians 5:24 agrees: "The one who calls you is faithful and he will do it."

Our salvation is secured not by our feeble grasp on God but by his strong grip on us. The ability to believe comes not from ourselves but from the Holy Spirit (John 3:6). Otherwise we would have no hope, no power for life. Yet, we have a choice of whether or not to receive and obey his Word to us, just as Sarah and Abraham did, when we are confronted with the reality of our human limitations and God's limitless love. For them the circumcision of Isaac, and later Abraham's willingness to sacrifice his son if God commanded it, sealed the covenant. Today, as then, God asks for the circumcision of our hearts, not just our bodies (Deut. 30:6). In faith and in action, we should strive to cut ourselves off from sin and cling to the cross.

The recognition of God's authority and Sarah's response of obedience were essential prerequisites to the arrival of Isaac, the promised seed. There is another aspect of Sarah's submission that is important for us to consider: the relationship between husband and wife. Peter points to Sarah as a model:

> Wives, in the same way be submissive to your husbands so that, if any of them do not believe the word, they may be won over without talk by the behavior of their wives. . . . Your beauty should not come from outward adornment, such as braided hair and the wearing of gold jewelry and fine clothes. Instead, it should be that of your inner self, the unfading beauty of a gentle and quiet spirit, which is of great worth in God's sight. For this is the way the holy women of the past who put their hope in God used to make themselves beautiful. They were submissive to their own

husbands, like Sarah, who obeyed Abraham and called him her master. You are her daughters if you do what is right and do not give way to fear (1 Peter 3:1–6).

The issue of submission is as relevant for A.D. 2000 as it was nearly 2000 years before Christ. Actually, I am not convinced that when Sarah called Abraham "my master" in Genesis 18:12 she was speaking with only pure love and respect in her voice. There was at least a tinge of sarcasm there. Nor can I believe that it was right for Sarah to submit in silence to Abraham when he resorted to expedience out of fear and first told a pharaoh in Egypt and then Abimelech, king of Gerar, that Sarah was his sister. But it is interesting to note a difference in their relationship before and after God confronted Sarah with his personal, powerful, probing presence in the face of her need (Gen. 18). When they were acting outside of God's will (Gen. 16), Sarai blamed Abram for the failure of her scheme, and he gave Hagar into her hands. Persecution of the servant resulted. After the birth of Isaac, there was a different outcome of their discussion concerning Hagar:

> The child grew and was weaned, and on the day Isaac was weaned Abraham held a great feast. But Sarah saw that the son whom Hagar the Egyptian had borne to Abraham was mocking, and she said to Abraham, "Get rid of that slave woman and her son, for that slave woman's son will never share in the inheritance with my son Isaac." The matter distressed Abraham greatly because it concerned his son. But God said to him, "Do not be so distressed about the boy and your maidservant. Listen to whatever Sarah tells you, because I will make the son of the maidservant into a nation also, because he is your offspring" (Gen. 21:8–13).

This time Abraham was encouraged to listen to his wife's advice because she was sensitive and submissive to God's will. Protection resulted for both sons and for Sarah as well, as her obedience to God increased her influence for good with her husband.

Each individual is accountable to God for the measure and nature of his or her obedience in every situation. Sarah's example challenges me to know and obey God, who knows me perfectly, so that in his power I can walk before him and be blameless and fruitful. I want to cooperate with my husband so that together we can discern God's will and go his way as a family. Then I am truly Sarah's daughter, as well as her namesake, if I "do what is right and do not give way to fear."

How might fearing for your personal safety or guarding what brings you satisfaction overshadow your faith and joy in your loving Savior? When God speaks to you, do you respond with the laughter of reverent submission, or the laughter of rebellion? In what ways is your relationship to the important people in your life a reflection of your obedience to God?

5

Esther

Primary Scripture Reading	Supplementary References
Book of Esther	Deuteronomy 30:1–6
	Psalms 25, 27, 37, 62
	Matthew 22:15–21
	1 Timothy 2:1–4
	Hebrews 13:17
	1 Peter 2:13–17

Questions for Study and Discussion

1. Read the entire Book of Esther. Why, do you think, is God's name not mentioned in it?

   Trace proofs of his presence and power behind the scenes.

   How are you aware of his control over seeming coincidences in your life?

2. What is your attitude toward the law of the land? Do you obey it perfectly (including all traffic and tax laws)?

Is there a time when you feel you need not or ought not obey the law? What guidelines do the above New Testament passages offer?

3. Why did Queen Vashti defy the king's command?

What personal rights do you claim? Whose rights have you stood up for, and with what results?

How do you feel about a husband's right to be "ruler over his own household" (Esther 1:22)?

4. What risks did Esther face in choosing to obey God's call? What risks were there in refusing?

How do you evaluate the risks of alternatives you face?

5. When and why have you kept secret your identity as a Christian (see Esther 2:20)?

Did your action bring either honor or dishonor to God? What did you learn from the experience?

6. Why did God allow Esther, a beautiful and believing Jewish virgin, to be taken into the harem of a pagan despot? How do Genesis 50:9–10 and 2 Corinthians 4 help you understand God's character and methods at work to accomplish his purposes in unusual ways (see also Isa. 55:8–11)?

How is God using circumstances of your life for training or blessing yourself and other people, which might be similar to the way he brought Esther to the palace "for such a time as this" (Esther 4:14)?

7. What do you know of God's perfect timing to accomplish his will as you have waited for him?

What do you think of Esther's strategy to expose Haman?

How do you balance patience with action as you seek to serve God in obedience (consider Pss. 25, 27, 37, and 62)?

*R*uth's obedience was a sincere and beautifully attractive expression of her love for Naomi and for her God. Sarah's obedience was sealed by God's powerful, personal confrontation, which transformed her natural dependence on her own resources into a deep faith in his power alone. In Esther's story we have an opportunity to consider obedience toward the law, as well as in marriage and family relationships. We shall consider the requirement, the risk, and the reward of obedience, both for Esther and for ourselves.

The Book of Esther is a holiday story. Each year at the Jewish Festival of Purim in late winter, the special scroll, or *Megillah*, is read in the synagogue. Every time the name of Haman, the villain, is mentioned, the whole congregation responds by hissing, and whirring raucous noisemakers called greggors. There is a joyous carnival atmosphere, with costume parades, games, and a sense of exhilaration as the story of the triumph of good over evil is retold. Family members exchange gifts, and baskets of food are brought to the poor, both in accordance with the details of the celebration decreed in Esther 9:22. Purim has no counterpart on the Christian calendar. But underneath the jubilation of special songs, traditional foods (triangular fruit-filled tarts called *hamantaschen*, or Haman's hats), and religious services, a tense drama is replayed, in which the heroine Esther saved her exiled people from total annihilation in the sixth century B.C.

Requirements of Obedience

Notice first the expectation of subservience in the social and legal context of Esther's day. Everyone in the empire had to obey the king of the Medes and Persians, Xerxes (or Ahasuerus), without question or delay. He himself was subject only to the law of the Medes and Persians, which could never be altered. When Queen Vashti refused to display herself in front of King Xerxes' banquet guests, she broke the law by defying his command. Such a violation threatened the whole system. In persuading him to take the severest possible action against her, his counselors expressed another fear:

> "For the queen's conduct will become known to all the women, and so they will despise their husbands and say,

'King Xerxes commanded Queen Vashti to be brought before him, but she would not come.' This very day the Persian and Median women of the nobility who have heard about the queen's conduct will respond to all the king's nobles in the same way. There will be no end of disrespect and discord" (Esther 1:17–18).

As long ago as 2500 years, there was considerable anxiety concerning a husband's authority and his wife's obedience within the home. These nobles made sure that dispatches were circulated to every province and in every language, proclaiming each man to be ruler over his own household. We do not know whether or not the directive achieved its purpose, but we can see that the question of obedience in marriage, which is also critical in our society, is hardly a new one.

We can also see the emphasis on obedience to the law. Besides the human actors in the Book of Esther, the law of the Medes and Persians played a crucial role in the drama. Evolved over a period of centuries as the Persian Empire gained supremacy over more and more territory (to the point of encompassing 127 provinces from India to Ethiopia by Esther's time), this legal system was ironclad. Every person in the empire was only too well aware of the dire consequences of violating its decrees, yet it was so complex that nearly everyone could be found guilty of some infraction. Once a decree was issued, it might never be amended or revoked, not even by the king himself. (This law of the Medes and Persians made a lot of trouble for Daniel, too. See Daniel 6, for example.) It was this law that sealed Queen Vashti's doom and that Haman tried to invoke to eliminate all the Jews. Fortunately, Haman's plan was thwarted by a higher law.

In reference to this higher law, it is curious that God's name is not mentioned once in the Book of Esther. Writers generally offer two reasons for this omission. Remember that the events of Esther occurred during the period of the Babylonian exile, which followed the defeat of Jerusalem in 586 B.C. This was a very low moment in Jewish history, when God's positive involvement in the lives of his people might have seemed both less apparent and less appreciated than during times of conquest. It is possible that some Jews found it easier to imagine that God was either impotent to help or else that he had abandoned them, and they chose to drop his name from their conversations and writings, rather than to face the fact that God had warned them specifically and repeatedly of the inevitable outcome of their continued disobedience to his law (see Deut. 30:1–6). But in fact, the tone of the Book of Esther is one of joy and victory, even at times of great fear and stress. God was not helpless, nor did he refuse to help.

A better explanation is that the omission of God's name was precautionary. The book closes with the Jews still in exile, safe but not free, with no assurance of when they might return to their homeland. They were wise to rejoice without seeming to gloat over their success, lest new plots arise against them. Persecution at the hands of stronger and more numerous enemies was always a possibility, and in fact proved to be a reality too often in Jewish history. What is beautiful to realize—and the pleasure is as real for believers today as it was for faithful Jews of Esther's day— is how mightily and mercifully God controlled events to care for his people both as individuals and as a nation, and how ultimately he received the glory by preserving his record in his Word.

A passage crucial to our considering God's requirement of obedience is Esther 4:13–16, which includes the appeal Esther's elder cousin Mordecai brought to her, and her response:

> "Do not think that because you are in the king's house you alone of all the Jews will escape. For if you remain silent at

this time, relief and deliverance for the Jews will arise from another place, but you and your father's family will perish. And who knows but that you have come to royal position for such a time as this?" Then Esther sent this reply to Mordecai: "Go, gather together all the Jews who are in Susa, and fast for me. Do not eat or drink for three days, night or day. I and my maids will fast as you do. When this is done, I will go to the king, even though it is against the law. And if I perish, I perish."

The first principle to realize is that God gives every individual choices. He does not manipulate anyone into accomplishing his purposes against his or her will. The Lord has much to teach and to give us, but he waits until we are willing to learn and receive it. Second, we should count it a great privilege to serve him in the ways he directs us, but we must also recognize that he is never helpless, whether or not he has our help. If we refuse the opportunity to obey, he will simply achieve his plans through someone else. His will *shall* be done, but we will miss the blessing. Mordecai made this point clear to Esther when he stated that her family would perish if she remained silent, while God would still send relief from another place. The potential loss was consequence enough for Esther, who took the risk of presenting herself before the king without being summoned, an act that demanded the death penalty according to the law of the Medes and Persians.

Risk of Obedience

Esther dared to approach the king uninvited. How did she become queen in the first place? Vashti had taken a risk also, by standing up for her rights and refusing to appear when the king had summoned her. Apparently, it was nearly as dangerous not to come when invited as to come uninvited! Vashti summarily lost her position for the sake of her principles. We should take a moment to consider whether she was right in the stand she took. She dared to insist on being treated with respect as an individual person of value, and not merely as one more bauble among the king's vast treasures to be displayed. It is difficult for us today to identify with the circumstances of her culture, yet I suppose that Vashti would undoubtedly receive sympathetic support for her ideals, if not for her actions, even though she lost her case in the court. Vashti's example deserves some attention, if not a separate chapter of study. Is hers the kind of self-expression for which we should be striving? Is it our rights or God's righteousness for which we must take a stand? In this book we are studying the women of the Old Testament in order to understand ourselves in the context of God's principles and possibilities. If we come to know who we are—individuals created in his image and for his glory—we shall develop a better sense of which rights are worth defending. What are you willing to risk, and for what purpose?

King Xerxes was not entirely pleased with the course of action he had followed in dealing with Queen Vashti. Several years later, after losing a war with Greece (historically placed between chapters 1 and 2 of Esther), he remembered with regret the events that led to the loss of his queen. But the law of the Medes and Persians gave him no option by which to restore her to his side. To cheer him a grand beauty contest was announced throughout the kingdom, with the winner to be declared the new queen. The beautiful young Jew Esther was chosen as a candidate and placed in the preliminary harem at Susa, the capital of the kingdom. She immediately gained the favor of the eunuch Hegai, manager of the harem, who saw to it that she received all the benefits of special food and beauty treatments during the twelve months of preparation for her one-night tryst with the king.

During that time, however, Esther was careful to obey Mordecai's orders not to disclose her identity as a Hebrew. In fact, Esther 2:20 indicates the extent to which obedience was a lifelong trait of this maiden:

> But Esther had kept secret her family background and nationality just as Mordecai had told her to do, for she continued to follow Mordecai's instructions as she had done when he was bringing her up.

Verse 7 explains that Mordecai had become Esther's guardian when her parents died some years earlier. Thus he represented the extent of Esther's family ties. She was already accustomed to obeying his wise and loving commands without question, trusting him to guide her.

Mordecai had a keen perception of whom and when to obey. He had uncovered and reported a plot to assassinate the king, an act of loyalty that was duly recorded and later rewarded. As a Jew, however, he had stoutly refused to bow down in homage to any man. This refusal so enraged the prime minister Haman that he swore to destroy not only Mordecai but every Jew in the kingdom. Mordecai's counsel to Esther when she entered the harem was not that she should resist the flow of events that would bring her to the king's bed, but that she should preserve the secret of her identity until the most advantageous time for her people and for herself. Mordecai was not a rebel. He was willing to abide by and support the system of government under which he lived, especially in order to achieve the protection of his people. But he had to take a stand against human authority when it infringed upon his primary obligation to obey God, his supreme authority. For that he would take any risk, and he encouraged Esther to do the same.

The turning point in Esther's story came as she chose to accept and fulfill the obligation of obedience to God. Once Mordecai opened Esther's eyes to the danger and the duty facing her, and to the critical role she could play in behalf of her people, she acted decisively to conceive and carry out her plan. Her first step was to call for a three-day fast of all the Jews in Susa. Well aware that she would be breaking the civil law, she asked her people to petition God to overrule that law with his divine protection. She placed herself in the hands of the highest authority, risking all to obey him. We would do well not only to admire, but also to apply Esther's process of patience, prayer, and planning as she carried out her purpose under God.

Seeing Esther move through the precarious schedule of invitations, petitions, and revelations recorded in chapters 5–8 of the story, we must be impressed with her poise and strength derived from her decision to rely on God and speak boldly for her people. She made no brash demands, issued no statements of defiance, and threw no fits of hysteria. Her beauty, calm, and sincere respect continued to attract the king, who was most eager to discover and fulfill the desire of her heart. She offered hospitality to Xerxes and Haman the second time and waited confidently for God to show her the perfect moment and manner in which to expose her news and her need—that Haman had twisted the inviolable law of the Medes and Persians to serve his own vanity by ordering the annihilation of the entire Jewish population. Esther was not set on challenging the authority of her king and husband. Her mission was much more urgent—to work within her proper position of queen to rescue her people. Her courage and faith in God empowered her to succeed where other methods and motives would surely have collapsed in failure.

Can you triumph in your situation by means of a solid confidence that God has indeed appointed you to serve him in your place at "such a time as this"? Will you put your faith in his ability to guide and strengthen you with his wisdom and love? In what ways do you need to grow in discernment regarding when to submit to those in authority over you and when to act boldly, always in obedience to God's principles rather than in service of your own pride? Esther's example provides a beautiful model to encourage and challenge each of us.

Reward for Obedience

Because Esther's cause was just, her timing perfect, and her God omnipotent, she accomplished her goal. Haman's wicked plot to hang Mordecai and murder all of the Jews came down on his own head, for he was hanged on the same gallows he had prepared for his enemy. The law now authorized the Jews to defend themselves against their would-be attackers on the specified days of slaughter. While they took revenge, however, they refused to take plunder from the Persians, in acknowledgment of God's help. Thus, the days Haman had chosen for their deaths they dedicated to joyful feasting and celebration—from that time to the present. The king elevated Mordecai to a position of greatness, and Esther was recognized as a sensitive and wise ruler along with her husband, to the great relief of all her people. The Book of Esther ends exuberantly:

> Mordecai the Jew was second in rank to King Xerxes, preeminent among the Jews, and held in high esteem by his many fellow Jews, because he worked for the good of his people and spoke up for the welfare of all the Jews (Esther 10:3).

The immediate results of Esther's obedience were indeed remarkable and are certainly worthy of annual celebration, even in our own day. But I believe she enjoys further honor by pointing the way for us to determine practical principles of obedience in our own lives, whenever we feel bound by uncomfortable constraints of a rigid chain of command. Esther could have felt caught between the social expectations to obey her cousin Mordecai on the one hand and her husband Xerxes on the other; or between the king of the Medes and Persians and the king of heaven and earth. Is it possible to follow a right course among such seemingly conflicting demands today? Esther's story shows us the possibility of an affirmative answer. She met such a challenge with quiet and consistent courage. She challenges us to persevere in our circumstances, focusing on God's purposes "for such a time as this," for the blessing of others as well as for our personal benefit. Instead of experiencing frustration and conflict over the constraints in our lives, we may discover that God's righteous requirement of obedience offers the rewards of rest and redemption if we are willing to place our faith wholly in him.

6

Hannah

Primary Scripture Reading

1 Samuel 1–2

Supplementary References

Numbers 6:1–21
Psalm 84:3

Questions for Study and Discussion

1. Describe Hannah's household. What was her relationship
   with Elkanah? Who was Peninnah?

   stressed

   How did Elkanah and Peninnah either encourage or pro-
   voke Hannah? For how long?

2. When and why was Hannah most unhappy?

   What did she do about her deep sorrow? How did the priest
   Eli respond to her behavior in 1 Samuel 1:10–18? When did
   Hannah stop praying? Why?

   she prayed, Eli thought she was drunk
   He stopped her, questioned her, then blest her

   What impresses you most about this passage? *Instead of patronizing*
   her

   maybe she had a prayer language
   she never gave up faith

3. Read Numbers 6:1–21. What are the requirements and purposes of a Nazirite vow? *grow long hair — outward sign of consecration*

Was Hannah trying to bargain with God, or was she proving her expectant faith by her vow?

Have you ever made a vow to God? Could you tell about the circumstances and the results? *baptise children, marraige vows*

4. Why did Hannah name her baby Samuel? *it means "I've asked him of the Lord" — God answered prayer*

What do you think about her actions in 1 Samuel 1:21–28? What was the hardest moment in her commitment? *leaving him*

From what you know of Eli's and Samuel's later history, as well as from these early chapters of the book, would you admire or criticize Hannah for leaving her son at the house of the Lord?

5. What attributes of God are mentioned in Hannah's prayer (1 Sam. 2:1–10)? In what ways are humans to respond to God, according to these verses? *No one besides you Rock holds life in his hands*

What connection do you find between the content of Hannah's prayer and the circumstances of her life at this time?

grateful of having had a son

6. Compare Hannah's action in bringing Samuel to the house of the Lord with the attitude expressed in Psalm 84:3. As a parent, how could you fully commit your offspring to God and still fulfill your responsibility to raise them?

What was unique about Hannah's performance of her role as a mother that demonstrates her strong faith?

7. In which ways was Hannah blessed by God for her faith?

How does her example encourage your faith in God in your difficult circumstances today?

Hannah was barren in an age in which conception of children was perceived to be a sign of God's blessing as well as being a practical protection of one's future rights and property. Not long after Hannah's time, Solomon wrote, "Sons are a heritage from the LORD, children a reward from him. Like arrows in the hands of a warrior are sons born in one's youth. Blessed is the man whose quiver is full of them" (Ps. 127:5). On the other hand, a lack of offspring was viewed not only as a serious threat to one's security but also as a direct punishment from the Lord. Vestiges of the same feelings and societal expectations remain today.

Hannah's failure to provide offspring was even more painful because her husband Elkanah had another wife, Peninnah, who would not let her forget the fact for a moment.

> Peninnah had children, but Hannah had none. Year after year this man [Elkanah] went up from his town to worship and sacrifice to the LORD Almighty at Shiloh, where Hophni and Phinehas, the two sons of Eli, were priests of the LORD. Whenever the day came for Elkanah to sacrifice, he would give portions of the meat to his wife Peninnah and to all her sons and daughters. But to Hannah he gave a double portion because he loved her, and the LORD had closed her womb. And because the LORD had closed her womb, her rival kept provoking her in order to irritate her. This went on year after year. Whenever Hannah went up to the house of the LORD, her rival provoked her till she wept and would not eat (1 Sam. 1:2–7).

Elkanah was aware of Peninnah's constant cruelty, and he tried to do something about it by saying to Hannah, "Hannah, why are you weeping? Why don't you eat? Why are you downhearted? Don't I mean more to you than ten sons?" (1 Sam. 1:8). He was probably just trying to be helpful, but Elkanah was not very sensitive. At best we can read his questions as a magnanimous gesture of comfort and a further demonstration of his sincere love for Hannah (in addition to his provision of a double portion of meat at the sacrifice, v. 5). At worst they may sound rather self-centered and unsympathetic. In either case, his questions failed to penetrate to the real problem or to point the way to a solution.

Prayer

It does not appear that Hannah had sought Elkanah's help or comfort, nor did she seem annoyed at his conceit. There was a solution to her problem, Hannah knew, but it did not begin with her husband. Instead,

> In bitterness of soul Hannah wept much and prayed to the LORD. And she made a vow, saying, "O LORD Almighty, if you will only look upon your servant's misery and remember me, and not forget your servant but give her a son, then I will give him to the LORD for all the days of his life, and no razor will ever be used on his head" (1 Sam. 1:10–11).

Over the next several verses, we are reminded of her intensity: "She kept on praying" (v. 12); "Hannah was praying in her heart" (v. 13); and, "I was pouring out my soul to the LORD. . . . I have been praying here out of my great anguish and grief" (vv. 15–16). Here, then, is the first indication of Hannah's faith. She took her deep troubles directly to God, trusting that he could, while others could not, provide a way of release from her distress.

Right now you, too, can choose to follow her example, and in the words of David, "Cast thy burden upon the LORD, and he shall sustain thee: he shall never suffer the righteous to be moved" (Ps. 55:22, KJV).

Promise

The actual content of Hannah's prayer deserves our careful attention. It followed the prescribed pattern of a Nazirite vow, which was ordained by God in Numbers 6:1–21:

> If a man or woman wants to make a special vow, a vow of separation to the LORD as a Nazirite, he must abstain from wine and other fermented drink and must not drink vinegar made from wine or from other fermented drink. He must

not drink grape juice or eat grapes or raisins. As long as he is a Nazirite, he must not eat anything that comes from the grapevine, not even the seeds or skins. During the entire period of his vow of separation no razor may be used on his head. He must be holy until the period of his separation to the LORD is over; he must let the hair of his head grow long. Throughout the period of his separation to the LORD he must not go near a dead body. . . . Throughout the period of his separation he is consecrated to the LORD. . . . This is the law of the Nazirite who vows his offering to the LORD in accordance with his separation, . . . He must fulfill the vow he has made, according to the law of the Nazirite.

This kind of vow represented a special provision by which a man or woman could consecrate himself or herself wholly to God for a specific purpose and for a limited period of time. After the conditions were fulfilled, careful instructions prescribed hair-shaving and sacrifices to signify God's acceptance of the vow and release from its constraints. In addition, any contact with a dead body while under vow constituted defilement, which necessitated total rededication of the vow. This meant recleansing, sacrificing, and starting the period of consecration over again. Finally, a person making such a vow was required to abstain from cutting the hair and from drinking wine. In short, the Nazirite vow was a serious transaction with the Lord; it represented a personal decision to become a "fragrant offering, an acceptable sacrifice, pleasing to God" (Phil. 4:18).

Critics have accused Hannah of wrongfully trying to bargain with God, because of the if—then clause in her promise. But rather than driving a bargain or trying to manipulate God, Hannah was dedicating herself wholly to him in faith by promising to return to his service the child whom she already believed he would provide. Keeping her end of the promise by sealing her commitment with a vow was a further important step in her journey of faith.

In the New Testament, Paul appears to have taken part in similar vows (Acts 18:18; 21:23–26). In John 15:19 and elsewhere, Jesus reminds us that he has chosen his own to be set apart, in the world but not of the world, for his service. How serious is your commitment to him?

The Nazirite vow was almost always initiated by an individual on his own behalf and for a limited period. But Hannah's vow consecrated her son to the Lord from the first anticipation of his conception through his entire lifetime. Samson and John the Baptist are the only other biblical examples of Nazirite vows pledged by parents (Judg. 13:5; Luke 1:15). In both cases, the command to consecrate these children was delivered by angels. What extraordinary commitment *by faith* shines through the mothers of each of these men!

Peace

Hannah was persistent and completely honest in expressing her desperate desire for a son. She did not leave her prayers until she felt sure that God had heard and would answer them. How do we know she received this assurance? When she finished her conversation with the priest Eli, who had observed and misunderstood the significance of her vow, he blessed her. "Eli answered, 'Go in peace, and may the God of Israel grant you what you have asked of him.' She said, 'May your servant find favor in your eyes.' *Then she went her way and ate something, and her face was no longer downcast*" (1 Sam. 1:17–18, italics added).

Here is the second mark of Hannah's faith. This turnabout of countenance was possible only because of her determination to *believe* that God *would* answer her need. She had not yet become pregnant, but she could eat and be cheerful *in faith*. Over and over again the psalms also express this same kind of radiant confidence in God: "In the day of my trouble I will call to you: for you will answer me" (Ps. 86:7; see also Pss. 56:3–4; 91:2; 138:7).

Do you exercise this determination to trust in God's help even before you see the end product? Throughout his Word, God continually invites us to *test* his promises in faith, so that we can praise him when he overwhelms us with his blessings.

> This poor man called, and the LORD heard him; he saved him out of all his troubles. The angel of the Lord encamps around those who fear him, and he delivers them. Taste and see that the Lord is good; blessed is the man who takes refuge in him (Ps. 34:6–8).

> "Bring the whole tithe into the storehouse, that there may be food in my house. Test me in this," says the LORD Almighty, "and see if I will not throw open the floodgates of heaven and pour out so much blessing that you will not have room enough for it" (Mal. 3:10).

There is a note of warning here, as well. To test God with an attitude of unbelief—an expectation that he must perform at our command or for our convenience—is strictly forbidden (see Deut. 6:16; Matt. 4:7). The difference between the right and wrong kind of testing lies both in the attitude of the asker and in the results of prayer. Hannah's heart was right toward God, and he blessed her. We would do well to examine our own motives before we come to him in prayer.

The peace that Hannah evidenced in her restored appetite and appearance following Eli's blessing of her vow lasted until her son was born, and is reflected in the name she chose for him. "So in the course of time Hannah conceived and gave birth to a son. She named him Samuel, saying, 'Because I asked the LORD for him'" (1 Sam. 1:20). The name Samuel sounds like the Hebrew word for *heard of God*. In naming her son, Hannah honored the Lord for hearing and answering her prayers. Here is another lesson in faith for us. In addition to believing that God would do what she had asked, she did not forget to praise him for hearing her prayers.

God delights in giving his children the desires of their hearts. And, like any parent, he likes to be appreciated. When Jesus healed ten lepers, only one returned to thank him.

> Jesus asked, "Were not all ten cleansed? Where are the other nine? Was no one found to return and give praise to God except this foreigner?" Then he said to him "Rise and go, your faith has made you well" (Luke 17:17–19).

Hannah's expression of thankfulness was a further demonstration of the peace she experienced within.

Praise

Once Hannah had made her vow she was no longer sad, but she had yet to fulfill her vow. In one sense, having made the solemn commitment, she had set a determined course to dedicate her son, and therefore may have gained strength through discipline to carry it to completion. "Once begun is half done" is a familiar adage. However, we know from our own experience that it is often much harder to *do* a thing than simply talk about it (like losing weight or reforming a bad habit). The remainder of 1 Samuel 1 and 2 allows us to glimpse Hannah at critical moments: she conceived, gave birth, refused to go to Shiloh until Samuel was weaned, brought him to the house of the Lord and entrusted him to Eli, and brought her son a new coat each year when she visited him. Did she show any signs of regret or wavering in her self-assigned promise? Nothing but joy radiates through this scene of her bringing Samuel to Eli:

After he was weaned, she took the boy with her, young as
he was, along with a three-year-old bull, an ephah of flour
and a skin of wine, and brought him to the house of the
LORD at Shiloh. When they had slaughtered the bull, they
brought the boy to Eli, and she said to him, "As surely as
you live, my lord, I am the woman who stood here beside
you praying to the LORD, I prayed for this child, and the LORD
has granted me what I asked of him. So now I give him to
the LORD. For his whole life he will be given over to the LORD."
And he worshipped the LORD there (1 Sam. 1:24–28).

In addition to these details, Hannah's beautiful psalm of
praise is also recorded for us:

Then Hannah prayed and said:
"My heart rejoices in the LORD;
    in the LORD my horn is lifted high.
My mouth boasts over my enemies,
    for I delight in your deliverance.

"There is no one holy like the LORD;
    there is no one besides you;
    there is no Rock like our God.

"Do not keep talking so proudly
    or let your mouth speak such arrogance,
for the LORD is a God who knows,
    and by him deeds are weighed.

"The bows of the warriors are broken,
    but those who stumbled are armed with strength.
Those who were full hire themselves out for food,
    but those who were hungry hunger no more.
She who was barren has borne seven children,
    but she who has had many sons pines away.

"The LORD brings death and makes alive;
    he brings down to the grave and raises up.

The Lord sends poverty and wealth;
    he humbles and he exalts.

He raises the poor from the dust
    and lifts the needy from the ash heap;
he seats them with princes
    and has them inherit a throne of honor.

"For the foundations of the earth are the Lord's;
    upon them he has set the world.
He will guard the feet of his saints,
    but the wicked will be silenced in darkness.

"It is not by strength that one prevails;
    those who oppose the Lord will be shattered.
He will thunder against them from heaven;
    the Lord will judge the ends of the earth.

Many authors have pointed out similarities between this prayer and Mary's psalm of praise at the Annunciation (compare Luke 1:46–55).

What was it that enabled Hannah to fulfill her promise with such poise and praise, rather than anxiety and mourning over having to part from the child she had desired for so long? There is only one explanation. Her deep, living faith gave Hannah the assurance that God had heard and answered her prayers, and that he was fully able to protect, guide, and use Samuel for his glory. Although some people have criticized this mother for abandoning her young child to the influence of the old priest and his wicked sons (Eli's bad example is sometimes blamed for Samuel's later difficulties with his own sons—see 1 Sam. 8:1–5), I view her action and her attitude as evidence of her solid conviction that she was actually entrusting Samuel to the Lord himself, who could oversee and over-rule in every human situation.

Provision

Hannah made and kept her promise to God in faith.
Every year she made a coat for Samuel and brought it to
him when she visited him at Shiloh (1 Sam. 2:19). She did
not try to forget about this child whom she had given to
the Lord. Rather, she continued to provide what she could
for him while he served in the better place appointed by
God for him. We also want to see that God kept his
promises to Hannah throughout this beautiful story. The
Nazirite vow seemed to be initiated by Hannah, but God
honored his part of the commitment and added further
blessings to her request. Every year Eli prayed for Elkanah
and his wife, saying,

> "May the LORD give you children by this woman to take the
> place of the one she prayed for and gave to the LORD." Then
> they would go home. And the LORD was gracious to Han-
> nah; she conceived and gave birth to three sons and two
> daughters. Meanwhile, the boy Samuel grew up in the pres-
> ence of the LORD (1 Sam. 2:20–21).

God did more for Hannah than simply provide a son
who would be returned to his own service. He gave her
peace and purpose and greater productivity than she had
any reason to expect. And he kept Samuel in his presence.
Surely he is worthy of the feeble responses we make to his
abundant blessings.

Not every mother is asked to dedicate her child to full-
time Christian ministry, nor should it be so. But we are
asked to give our children fully into God's care for whatever particular purpose he has designed, and to dedicate
them joyfully to it, whatever the distance or cost. Even if
we have no physical offspring, we can dedicate ourselves
wholeheartedly as children of God. Indeed, such total commitment is a privilege, and it brings blessing (2 Chron.
16:9).

Hannah's faith ministered to me several years ago when, much to my surprise, I found myself in tears on the night before my son's first day of kindergarten. Even though I had thought I was looking forward to that day for many months, and though I had prepared him for it with anticipation of new clothes, friends, and adventures, I discovered I was obviously still unwilling to deposit him irrevocably on that doorstep of independence and learning known as school. Then I was moved to remember Hannah's example. She never showed such ambivalence. She had cherished all along the thought that I only recalled in the morning: God would *always* be with her son, even where and when she could not go with him. I imagined that she prayed constantly for her little boy while they were separated, and I could and would do the same for mine.

Soon after my experience I discovered another verse which I frequently claim as a reminder to myself that my children are always more secure in God's hands than in mine: "Yea, the sparrow hath found an house, and the swallow a nest for herself, where she may lay her young, even thine altars, O Lord of hosts, my King, and my God" (Ps. 84:3, KJV).

Knowing this truth, what better option could Hannah choose than to entrust her son to God in his house and rejoice? Do you share her joy, so that you, too, wholeheartedly entrust your family and future to him?

2 Ki 4:8, 12, 16,
20, 27, 36

Shunam - a town
of Issachar →
son of Jacob + Leah
Ge 30:18, 35:23, 49:14
Jos 19:17

7

Shunammite Woman

Primary Scripture Reading

2 Kings 4 and 8

Supplementary References

Luke 4:14–15
Philippians 3:12–14
Hebrews 4:15–16

Questions for Study and Discussion

1. What was the situation of the Shunammite woman? What did she do for Elisha? *built him a room*

   Did she have an ulterior motive for her action? *perhaps*

2. What did Elisha offer to do for her? How did she respond? *give her a child* *She said no*

   What emotions underlay her reaction? *too old, fear of an impossible feat*

3. What assumptions was Gehazi making in 2 Kings 4:14? *that she wanted a son or a younger husband*

   Why did the Shunammite protest in 4:16? *fear of being mislead*

What did she mean when she quoted herself in 4:28?

I told you so

4. List the full sequence of events following the boy's death. Why was the Shunammite evasive toward her husband and Gehazi? Did she deliberately lie to them?

What differences do you observe between those two men and Elisha?

5. Find the approximate distance from Shunem to Mount Carmel. At what point in her journey would you say the woman's faith and patience were most sorely tried? Why?

6. How was the Shunammite rewarded for her persistent faith in 2 Kings 4? How in 2 Kings 8?   *she got her land*
life of her son   *her house*
                                                           + her income

Have you experienced either kind of miracle? In what ways have you been persistent?

How can you use the Shunammite's story to activate your faith?

7. If a true prophet of God offered to perform some service for you, what would you ask for?

What is keeping you from expressing your heart's desire to God himself right now? Spend a few moments in honest, expectant prayer.

*T*hroughout his ministry, the prophet Elisha exercised tremendous power and authority from God to prophesy and perform miracles. Among the many individuals to whom he ministered, the well-to-do woman of Shunem stands out as a beautiful testimony to dynamic faith. This unnamed woman's preparation and persistence enabled her to experience God's providential power in a unique way. Her perception of God's character and her personality challenge us to expect God to meet our needs when we place our faith wholly in him.

Preparation

The Shunammite's preparation for Elisha provides the first evidence of her faith. In 2 Kings 4:8, she began by urging him to stay for one meal. Her hospitality must have been both gracious and delicious; Elisha readily became a regular guest whenever he came by. Soon the woman proposed to her husband that they build a special room for Elisha, explaining, "I know that this man who often comes our way is a holy man of God" (2 Kings 4:9).

The fact that the woman recognized Elisha as a prophet suggests both his considerable reputation and her own ready faith. Her motive was genuine. Although she was well aware of the stature of her guest, she offered him her hospitality in service to God and not as a means of obtaining any credit or recognition for herself. There is no hint of her boasting or gossiping to friends about her famous guest, or appealing to him for special favors. For his part, Elisha obviously appreciated both the meals and the restful haven she provided in her home. His offer to render some service to her (2 Kings 4:13) derived in turn from his sincere gratitude, not from any sense of obligation.

In considering the quality of the Shunammite's preparation, will you first examine your own motives? Is your hospitality offered in service to God only, or do you secretly hope to gain some other direct or indirect benefit from it? Jesus warned:

> "When you give a luncheon or dinner, do not invite your friends, your brothers or relatives, or your rich neighbors; if you do, they may invite you back and so you will be repaid. But when you give a banquet, invite the poor, the crippled, the lame, the blind, and you will be blessed. Although they cannot repay you, you will be repaid at the resurrection of the righteous" (Luke 14:12–15).

It is interesting to notice Elisha's offer of service to the Shunammite: "Can we speak on your behalf to the king or the commander of the army?" (2 Kings 4:13). He did not propose petitioning God in her behalf, even though his primary renown and duty were as a prophet and not as a royal or military confidant. Why did he limit his offer to the national rather than the spiritual realm, especially since the real desire of her heart (to have a child) could only be granted by God? Clearly, she recognized who he was; so he could not have been trying to conceal his identity or power. Could he have been evaluating her motives and her faith by giving her an opportunity to express her deep desire and to turn to God for help without Elisha's prompting? If so, did she fail or pass the test?

Prophecy

Without our knowing exactly what Elisha had in mind with his question, it is not easy to interpret the Shunammite's reply: "I have a home among my own people" (2 Kings 4:13). Why did she not simply tell Elisha of her deep longing for a child? Several reasons are suggested below, with some possible hidden attitudes in parentheses:

1. To have "a home among her own people" was fully satisfying to her. Her family's support had helped her withstand the prejudice of her culture against the childless. (Contentment, security)
2. She wanted a child, but she did not mention her desire because Elisha had only offered to speak to the king or commander, neither of whom could have helped in her situation. (Realism)
3. She wanted a child, but she did not feel that her own gesture of hospitality was sufficient to merit such a large blessing in return. She did not wish to bother the great prophet with her problems. (Humility)
4. She wanted a child, but she did not really believe that Elisha or even God himself had the power to grant her desire. (Doubt, lack of faith)
5. She wanted a child, but she felt that her barrenness was a judgment or punishment from God (in accordance with the beliefs of her culture), which even Elisha could not overturn. (Shame, disgrace)
6. She wanted a child, but she would not expose her private longing to further derision or disappointment. (Pride)
7. She accepted her childlessness as God's plan for her, so she was no longer "kicking against the goads"; this unmet desire was no longer a burning issue that needed to be brought up. (Peace)

Why did the Shunammite answer Elisha as she did? It is impossible to say with certainty which of the above explanations, or any others you may wish to offer, most accurately represent the true state of the Shunammite's feelings. Probably a combination of desires and fears was at work to keep her from talking freely with God's prophet about her yearning for a child.

It is well worth considering how we might respond to such an offer of assistance as Elisha made, and what underlying attitudes may be reflected in the thoughts we either express aloud or keep hidden within our hearts. Are we afraid to tell the Lord our innermost fears and hopes? He knows them all, whether we confess them or not. Do we trust him to deal gently and wisely with our very souls?

> For we do not have a high priest who is unable to sympathize with our weaknesses, but we have one who has been tempted in every way, just as we are—yet was without sin. Let us then approach the throne of grace with confidence, so that we may receive mercy and find grace to help us in our time of need (Heb. 4:15–16).

Although the Shunammite did not express it openly, it did not take long for Elisha, through his servant Gehazi, to discern her true desire: "Well, she has no son and her husband is old" (2 Kings 4:14). The almost desperate tone in her response to the prophet's promise of a son within the year proved the accuracy of Gehazi's perception. She protested, "No, my lord. Don't mislead your servant, O man of God!" (2 Kings 4:16). It is evident that her hesitation was only founded in the fear that Elisha's promise might not come to pass. Indeed, Elisha had prophesied the very event that she had desired most but had given up all hope of attaining.

Persistence

All went well for a few years. The Shunammite conceived and gave birth to a son the following year, as Elisha had foretold. We can readily imagine her boundless joy and praise to God for his unexpected blessing. But one morning, when the boy went out to his father in the fields, he suddenly cried out, "My head! My head!" and collapsed. He was carried to his mother's lap, where he sat until noon and then died. The mother's reaction is quite remarkable: no screams, no calls for help, no tears, no rending of clothes, nor even any effort to revive the child. Instead, "she went up and laid him on the bed of the man of God, then shut the door and went out" (2 Kings 4:21). As far as she was concerned, the boy's death was unacceptable; therefore, she refused to acknowledge it with any outward sign, either of panic or of mourning.

When tragedy strikes in our lives, isn't it a normal reaction to deny its existence, to shout out, "No! It isn't true!" and to try to erase the facts by the very volume of our cries? It requires all of our faith to accept such trials and at the same time claim and receive the full comfort of God's love in the midst of our grief. Then, especially, we must cling tightly to what we know of his character and his care, trusting his plan to be perfect even when we least understand it.

The Shunammite's crisis both strained and strengthened her faith. It drew her into a closer relationship with God, not through passive acceptance but through action. She was so certain that the Lord would not have promised and then provided a son, only to take him from her so soon, that she quietly laid him on the prophet's bed and set out to secure the only power that could effectively help in her situation. She understood that only God *could* restore her son, and she believed that he *would*. She had no need to tell God what to do, but, knowing what he would do, she acted forthrightly to claim the full amount of his blessing for her.

The rapid flow of events that followed the boy's death is a wonderful demonstration of faith in action. There was not a moment's indecision or delay. No time or word was wasted. No obstacle or distraction could sway her from her goal, which was to fetch Elisha to the bedroom she had provided for him, in order that he might restore her child to life.

Consider the individuals who in some way cluttered her path but were dispatched by her urgent authority.

Person	Obstruction (question/action)	Her Response
Husband	"Why go to him today? It's not the New Moon or the Sabbath."	"It's all right."
Servant/ Donkey		*She* saddled the donkey and said to her servant, "Don't slow down for me unless I tell you."
Gehazi	(Sent by Elisha to ask whether everything was all right)	"Everything is all right."
	Came over to push her away	Took hold of Elisha's feet
Elisha	But the man of God said, "Leave her alone! She is in bitter distress, but the LORD has hidden it from me and has not told me why." (Sent Gehazi with his staff to lay it on the boy's face)	"Did I ask you for a son, my lord?" she said. "Didn't I tell you, 'Don't raise my hopes'?"
	So he got up and followed her.	"As surely as the LORD lives and as you live, I will not leave you."

Many of us would say that we are sincerely seeking God's will for our lives, yet how casually we sometimes amble toward the goals his will prescribes. Do we know the difference between a goal and an obstacle? We must learn from the Shunammite's example to pursue God's promises with urgent confidence, letting no person or circumstance hinder our attainment of every glory for his name's sake.

The apostle Paul adds the spiritual as well as the practical aspect of this quest.

> Not that I have already obtained all this, or have already been made perfect, but I press on to take hold of that for which Christ Jesus took hold of me. Brothers, I do not consider myself yet to have taken hold of it. But one thing I do: Forgetting what is behind and straining toward what is ahead, I press on toward the goal to win the prize for which God has called me heavenward in Christ Jesus (Phil. 3:12–14).

Nothing should be permitted to dissuade, distract, or discourage us from obtaining this prize for ourselves. In spite of our present trials, we must realize the power and personality of God as well as the Shunammite woman did, so that we, too, may set our feet on course to attain the full measure of his promise. We must choose to know him better, through study and application of his Word, so that our lives may radiate such persistent faith as the Shunammite demonstrated.

Two other observations may be made from the chart above. First, the husband's objection, "Why go to him today? It's not the New Moon or the Sabbath" (2 Kings 4:23) reveals that his concept of seeking the Lord was limited to outward forms or ritual observances. He did not need God except in the performance of his religious obligations (compare Col. 2:16). His wife was quite different. She knew God more personally, through his servant Elisha, and she understood immediately that he alone could help in her desperate emergency. She sought God out of critical need, not ritual requirement, and he responded out of love.

Why do you worship? Do you attend church on Sundays because you feel you are supposed to? Or do you seek God's presence at all times because you must, since only he can "satisfy the desires of every living thing" (Ps. 145:16)?

The second point to notice is the nature and necessity of the Shunammite woman's journey. Why did she travel so far (about sixty miles for the round trip) and so fast (she left after the child died at noon, and presumably returned with Elisha before nightfall), when she could have asked the Lord directly to save her son?

To answer, we must keep in mind the historical setting of this story. In the age of the Old Testament prophets, God's power was manifest primarily through his particular appointed servants, who proclaimed his word and performed miracles in his name. This does not mean that God was ever inaccessible or indifferent to the needs or calls of any individual who turned to him for help. The Shunammite was aware and appreciative of God's personal interest in her family, and she responded personally to his promise of a child. Still, she was not able to experience the same kind of intimate relationship with the Lord that believers can enjoy today through the Holy Spirit. For her, Elisha represented God in word and deed, and she was convinced that only by bringing him physically to her child could she avail herself of God's power. Apparently, she was correct in her conclusion, since neither Elisha's servant nor his wooden staff sent in his absence had any effect on the boy. In fact, the woman's perceptions were even clearer than those of Elisha himself, who had to admit that the reason for her distress was at first hidden from him (2 Kings 4:27). He submitted to her demands because it was evident that she knew better than he what and how God would work in her situation. With our privilege of direct access to God through Christ when we pray today, we dare not become so complacent that we fail to avail ourselves of every comfort, guidance, and power he extends.

Preparation, Persistence, and Provision Repeated

In 2 Kings 8, we find a beautiful sequel to the Shunammite's story. Again we see her preparation as she obeyed
Elisha's instructions to "go away with your family and stay
wherever you can, because the LORD has decreed a famine
in the land that will last seven years" (2 Kings 8:1). When
she returned, she discovered that her house and land had
been confiscated. Again we see her persistence in coming
directly to the king to beg for the restoration of her property. And again we see God's perfect provision for her.

Obedience is the outward expression of inner faith. The
Shunammite who had already experienced first God's
promise through the prophet of a child and then his power
to restore the child to life, did not hesitate to believe Elisha's
prediction of famine and to obey his command to leave
the country. The simple statement, "The woman proceeded
to do as the man of God said" (2 Kings 8:2), is in marked
contrast to her earlier protest: "No, my lord. Don't mislead
your servant, O man of God!" (2 Kings 4:16), and demonstrates her growing faith. Of course, the nature of the second prophecy was quite different from the first one; instead
of touching her deepest personal desire, the famine was a
more general and external pronouncement of God's judgment against the entire nation. Even so, we can sense a
change in her attitude—greater regard for Elisha and deeper
reverence for God—which grew out of her previous experiences. It had not been wrong for her to question Elisha
on the earlier occasion, but her subsequent experience and
faith were such that she did not need to question him any
further. She simply obeyed. In what ways have your faith
and experience in the past prepared you to accept and obey
God's present commands to you?

Seven years elapsed, and the famine ended. The Shunammite, apparently a widow by this time, displayed the
same clear perception of her need, the same assessment of

resources, and the same decisiveness we observed in 2 Kings
4. As we saw her thrust aside every obstacle in order to reach
Elisha and bring him to her child, so now we see her persistence in cutting through the royal red tape to get directly
to the king with her request. It is not difficult to imagine
her refusing to be deterred or delayed by the many servants
and bureaucrats who cluttered the court; she proved her
boldness once again by daring to interrupt the king's conversation with Gehazi.

In pursuing what she knew to be hers by right, her persistence paid off once again, for the king responded by
instructing an official to "give back everything that
belonged to her, including all the income from her land
from the day she left the country until now" (2 Kings 8:6).
This command suggests that it may have been the king
himself who had possessed and profited from her land during her absence, as no other offender is named. In 1 Samuel
8:5 the Israelites demanded that Samuel appoint "a king
to lead us such as all the other nations have," and God
warned them that earthly kings would abuse them in various ways, including seizure of their best land (1 Sam. 8:14).
In the case of the Shunammite, at least, we find a king who
was willing to return the land with interest.

What readily persuaded this king to return the woman's
land, aside from the obvious rightness of her cause and his
own magnanimous spirit (or possibly his own guilty con-
science)? Once again, we note God's marvelous providence
in ordaining the "coincidence" by which the woman
arrived to plead her case at the exact moment when Gehazi
was recounting to the king the miracle of Elisha's restoration of her son some years before.

> The king was talking to Gehazi, the servant of the man of
> God, and had said, "Tell me about all the great things Elisha
> has done." Just as Gehazi was telling the king how Elisha
> had restored the dead to life, the woman whose son Elisha

had brought back to life came to beg the king for her house and land. Gehazi said, "This is the woman, my lord the king, and this is her son whom Elisha restored to life." The king asked the woman about it, and she told him (2 Kings 8:4–6).

The perfect timing of the Shunammite's arrival both confirmed Gehazi's story and assured the success of the woman's mission. Our eternal, omnipresent God seems to delight in ordering events within our finite time-and-space framework to accomplish his will and bring glory to his name. The Bible is filled with wonderful examples such as this one that demonstrate his timely provision for those who ask in faith for his help.

He provides for us in the same way today. It is as much a miracle when we recognize God's unseen hand moving within the natural world that he designed (see Rom. 8:28; Rev. 4:11) as when he performs some extraordinary work that seems to defy nature itself (e.g., when the sun stood still for Joshua, Josh. 10:13; Moses' leprosy, Exod. 4:6–7; and various restorations to life, 2 Kings 4, John 11:38–44).

The Shunammite's experiences demonstrate both types of provision: first, God's miraculous restoration of life to her dead son, through Elisha; and second, his perfect timing of her appeal to coincide with Gehazi's account of her story. Early in their friendship Elisha had offered to speak to the king in her behalf when she actually needed God's help (2 Kings 4:13). Now Elisha's influence was effective as the woman spoke to the king about what God had done. Her story blessed the king who in turn blessed her with the return of her property.

How do we react to "coincidences"? What miracles is God working in our lives right now? It is the Holy Spirit who makes us aware of God's providence in ordinary as well as extraordinary events, while we through grace increase in knowledge and sensitivity. The Shunammite woman triumphed because of her preparation by faith and obedience, her persistence to know and attain God's will, and her increasing experience of God's power and provision. To receive the greatest blessing from this short, simple story, each of us would do well to evaluate the depth of her own faith. Let the Shunammite challenge us and stir us to action.

Suggestions for Group Leaders

1. Keep in mind that the purpose of group discussion is to help all the members understand the Bible, implement the truths learned, refresh each other by exchanging thoughts, impressions, and ideas, and to support the formation of bonds of friendship.

2. Encourage the members to set aside a daily time for study and prayer.

3. Remind the members to write out answers. Expressing oneself on paper clarifies thoughts and analyzes understanding. Because written answers are succinct and thoughtful, discussion will be enlivened.

4. Be familiar enough with the lesson so you can identify questions that can most easily be omitted if time is short. Select and adapt an appropriate number of questions so that the lesson topic can be completed. Reword the question if the group feels it is unclear. Covering too little material is discouraging to the class. Skip the questions that cover material the class has already discussed. Often the last questions are the most thought-provoking. Choose questions that create lively and profitable interchange of views.

5. Encourage all members to participate. Often the less vocal people have amazingly thoughtful contributions.

6. Keep the group focused on the passage studied, emphasizing that answers should come from Scripture. Steer the discussion away from tangents. Side-step controversial subjects, Christian causes, political action, and so forth. Ask, "Where did you find that in this passage?" "Did anyone find a thought not yet mentioned?"

7. Pick up on any "live news" of spiritual growth, recent actions taken, honest admissions of inadequacy or failures, and desires for prayer. Be sensitive to "beginners" in the Christian walk, recognizing their need to share new discoveries, joys, commitments, and decisions.

8. Spend time in prayer as you prepare for the lesson. Remember to pray for each member. Pray daily for yourself to have a listening ear, a sensitive heart, and an effervescent and contagious spirit of joy as you lead. Pray you will affirm each member who contributes. Ask God to give you a variety of ways to do this.

Closing Remarks

Prepared closing remarks are valuable (and essential) for clearing up misunderstandings of the passage, further teaching, applying the Scripture to current situations, and for challenging each individual to action. Before the meeting decide on how much time to allow for discussion and closing remarks, and follow the timetable.